The Architecture of Student-Oriented Course Design

For Christopher and Rebecca

The Architecture of Student-Oriented Course Design

Building a Course for Contemporary Higher Education Students

Nicholas Jackson

Associate Professor of Organizational Behavior, Leeds University Business School, UK

Edward Elgar
PUBLISHING

Cheltenham, UK • Northampton, MA, USA

Published by
Edward Elgar Publishing Limited
The Lypiatts
15 Lansdown Road
Cheltenham
Glos GL50 2JA
UK

Edward Elgar Publishing, Inc.
William Pratt House
9 Dewey Court
Northampton
Massachusetts 01060
USA

A catalogue record for this book
is available from the British Library

Library of Congress Control Number: 2024936883

This book is available electronically in the **Elgar**online
Business subject collection
https://dx.doi.org/10.4337/9781035309559

MIX
Paper | Supporting
responsible forestry
FSC
www.fsc.org   FSC® C013604

ISBN 978 1 0353 0954 2 (cased)
ISBN 978 1 0353 0955 9 (eBook)

Printed and bound by CPI Group (UK) Ltd, Croydon, CR0 4YY

Contents

Figures

Tables

Boxes

Preface

Like me, you are probably just a humble academic trying to make your way in the world with a passion for making a difference to the lives of many who have entered the domain of post-compulsory education: a passion that will help to inspire students to learn and advance their knowledge of your discipline. While this is a worthy cause and provides good reason to dedicate so much of your time to planning, organizing, preparing, delivering, and assessing the student outcomes from your work of art, unfortunately, having a genuine passion is not enough. It is all too easy to overlook the amazing work you, and others like you, perform in the cause of advancing knowledge.

Before I launch into my book, let me begin by telling you a bit about myself, my credentials for writing a book of this nature, and my 'big idea' that inspired me to write the book in the first place. I am an Associate Professor of Organizational Behavior and I work for a UK university that was one of the founding members of what is known as the Russell Group of universities. However, as you may or may not already be aware, we academics tend to take up a variety of other roles, and in doing so I have also gained experience through being a mentor, personal tutor, head of year, program director, Director of Employability and Opportunity, and Director of Quality and Taught Programs at the Business School here in Leeds.

Having shared with you a few of my experiences as an academic, let me now explain how I have tried to harness that experience to develop an informed account of course and program design: an account that will help to support colleagues who are new to academia, but also a more experienced hand like me. In writing this book I have applied anecdotal evidence from my various practices of working and teaching in higher education, along with the evidence I have gleaned from the many interactions I have experienced with my colleagues. But I have also drawn from a wide body of published research in the field of higher education, and from theories of learning more generally.

While my key aim in writing this book has been to help and support colleagues with course development in the world of post-compulsory teaching, I would also dearly like to believe that an outcome of this work will be more-inspired students who are better equipped with the right kinds of skills they will need to enter the graduate workplace. There have been many changes in higher education over recent years and, as the general nature of the industry evolves, we must respond with more specific and targeted action that involves adapting the way we work with our students.

Yet, while recognizing a need to change the way we operate if we are to continue inspiring our students and to avoid more negative behaviors, such as low student engagement or dodging class attendance, the type of change we introduce needs to be informed change. My main objective in writing this book has not just been to propose better ways of developing our courses to engage and inspire confidence in our students, but also to help you understand why they may behave in a way that is not always conducive to learning. Let us refer to these as the antecedents of their inclination to disengage. Because if you are better informed about the causes of student behavior, you will also be better equipped to help mitigate the effects of withdrawal behaviors before they begin to emerge. Otherwise, these behaviors could have a detrimental impact on student performance and, potentially, escalate into issues with the rate of student attrition.

While writing this book I have tried to be all-encompassing and inclusive for the sake of academics working in an international context. However, depending on your global location, nuances often apply and so there are a few points I would like to highlight at this juncture. I have naturally been inclined to include examples from my own teaching and these relate to experiences in a Business School. Even so, I believe that most of my references to student experience and the psychology of students are generic to the experiences of those starting out and participating within the wider realms of higher education.

I would also like to point out that throughout this book I refer to both university programs and courses as separate entities. In this context, a program relates to the wider discipline of study the student will embark on (e.g., BA Fine Art; MSc Advanced Computer Science; Master of Business Administration). Dependent on the colloquialisms used in your corner of the world, the terms 'course' and 'module' can either be used interchangeably or have a very different interpretation.[1] For consistency and the avoidance of doubt, where I refer to a single taught component of the wider program, it is referred to in this book as a course.

There are a few people who I would like to thank for their support. First, I would like to thank the editorial team at Edward Elgar Publishing for their help and advice from the outset. They were kind enough to offer their expertise with each aspect of the writing process and I am very grateful for this.

Although I am sole author of this book, there are some people I have worked with along my journey to whom I will also be forever grateful. Without their advice and influence I would not have moved this project beyond the stage of it being merely an aspirational idea. Becoming an academic involves meeting a variety of inspirational people within the industry who will be able to offer support in various ways. As I have found (and I am sure you will too), this may be through their words of wisdom, straightforward (and sometimes blunt!) advice, or helping you to get your name out where it matters most within a challenging and competitive environment. Without meeting these people along the journey, I would not have had the opportunity to put my thoughts down on paper and write this book. In this respect, I owe them a very big thank you! More generally, I would like to thank Leeds University Business School for its support over the years while helping me to learn and grow as an academic. By writing this book I hope I can convey some of my experiences to those of you who are new to academia (or perhaps like me have been around a little while longer) and help support you on your own learning journey.

I hope you enjoy reading my book and find it helpful toward your teaching practice in higher education!

NOTE

1. For example, in the UK a single taught component of a higher education program is often referred to as a module rather than a course.

1. Introduction to *The Architecture of Student-Oriented Course Design: Building a Course for Contemporary Higher Education Students*

For all new students, the transition to university can be a challenging time. Earlier experiences of education are likely to differ, and the unfamiliar environment may offer more than a subtle contrast to the expectations students bring with them at the start of their university life. For the new recruits, this period of socialization involves transitioning to a more independent way of learning, and while many will arrive with this in mind, they are often ill-prepared for what it actually means. Taking responsibility for one's own learning can be a challenge for many students making the break from their experiences in secondary school or college (Cook and Leckey, 1999). Many undergraduates arrive at university straight from their home environment only several months after waving goodbye to all at the school gates. In most corners of their lives, dependency has been the operative form for most of these students and adapting to more distant and less supportive relationships is often where the unprepared come unstuck. Students familiar with a more supportive background may be able to comfortably meet the university entry requirements but might struggle academically when stepping into an independent learning environment.

Concern about the students' abilities to adjust to the different challenges of higher education is supported by some of the investigations relating to academic performance and student drop-out rates (attrition) during their first year of study. Evidence suggests that most undergraduate students who drop out of higher education do so in that first year (Paura and Arhipova, 2014), with one of the main reasons cited being a misalignment of their expectations and the reality of what is required of them to perform effectively within that environment. In contrast, students who are prepared to take more accountability for their own learning in the first year of study achieve higher marks than those who expect the lecturers and other teaching staff to shoulder more of the responsibility (Nicholson et al., 2013). Even so, where service delivery has been perceived as 'not meeting expectations', there has been a rise in student complaints. All this has been occurring at a time of increasing costs for students partaking in higher education and, consequently, for those providing financial support for their loved ones during their time at university.

In addition to some potentially uncomfortable truths about them adapting to their new environment, it is also helpful to understand your students' motivations when tempted to transition to university and when choosing their program of study. These are not inconsequential questions and, indeed, may establish why a student is struggling to settle into their environment. Often, these are the factors that underlie student attrition and can also impact the all-important attitude of engagement during the initial period of their program. While attrition levels may not be such a big problem for postgraduates in study, it is an issue for many undergraduate programs, particularly during the first year at university (Shcheglova et al., 2020). Uncertainty about motives and direction may also influence a student's identity with their program and their wider cohort, which can morph into issues with engagement and self-efficacy. Both the level of student engagement and the degree of self-efficacy will influence the quality of the student experience.

As educators, we have a critical role in shaping the student's experience during this early transition to higher education and the period beyond once socialization is complete. The contributions made by academic and professional staff during the welcome and induction program have an important part to play in the transition – not least, the emphasis placed on orienting students to each channel of support that will be available to them during this period and beyond. Because Semester 1 teaching begins so soon after the students arrive at university, it is inevitable that the first few weeks become an extension of the induction period as students barely have time to catch their breath. Therefore, guidance and direction offered by program directors, course leaders, and supporting teaching assistants will also be a critical element of this early experience for the student.

As either a program director or course leader, your role during this initial period of nervous energy and emotional tensions will be central to each of the students that you guide and direct, so do not underestimate the significance of your actions. Your course, its content, how it is structured, and your own delivery style will all impact the quality of the student experience in those important early days and beyond. The quality of the course design is linked to early student engagement, and so it will be vital that you get off to a good start. But it is also important to know something about the student psyche, considering the emotional experiences of the new student, particularly if they are starting a new chapter of their education. Course design will therefore play a crucial part in all of this.

One of my main objectives in authoring this book is to help academics, both those new to teaching and those who have been around a while longer, to plan and design a new course that considers the needs of the most important person: the student! From my experiences in education as a teacher, mentor, program director, and director of quality, programs, and employability, I will bring to the fore what I recognize as key factors that we should be including in our thoughts when planning and designing (or redesigning) a new course. Hopefully, this will make your course more interesting and thought-provoking, enabling you to reach out to your students by meeting both their needs and most, if not all, of their expectations.

I have split the book into two parts. Part I focuses on the world from a student perspective, arriving at university and beginning their new year of study. Here, I contemplate their range of potential motivations for starting out and what happens when expectation meets reality. I discuss the important contribution of human capital theory when reflecting on the rudimentary aims of the student and compare this to how we can help shape the student in our role as educators. Moving on, I discuss the problematic issues surrounding student confidence, what we as educators need to be aware of vis-à-vis self-efficacy, fear of failure, and making sure we are being inclusive in the design and delivery of our courses.

I also reflect on some of the challenges that appear when using a blended or hybrid approach to teaching and the distinct aspects you will need to consider when mixing face-to-face with online teaching where this is either appropriate or necessary. Building confidence moves seamlessly into maximizing student engagement through the critical phases of forming an identity with the course, the teaching staff, and peers. Inclusive practice, interaction with both peers and teaching staff, and the art of building the tutor–student relationship are all included in Chapter 4.

In the closing chapter of Part I, I move on to discuss the topic of skills and how to incorporate these into your course during the design phase, drawing links with the growth in confidence and engagement as your students are encouraged to develop their skills through active participation in class. I also discuss, in Chapter 5, both formative and summative assessment, recognizing how you can align these with the skills you are looking to develop.

The emphasis in Part II is all on design, and in some measure drawing on the student perspectives I discuss in Part I. So, in addition to illustrating measures you can take to help build student confidence, and enhance their engagement, I discuss a range of practical skills that can easily be incorporated into your teaching and will be of particular value to students as they begin to transfer into their post-academic worlds.

I conclude the text in Chapter 9, drawing together the main propositions I have outlined throughout Parts I and II. Hopefully, this book will help you reflect on your teaching practice, in whatever capacity you work as an educator, whether you are a course leader, a program director, or engaged in some other way with the critical process of course design.

PART I

The student perspective

2. Understanding the student psyche and wider motivations

2.1 TOO MANY CHOICES

Like me, I am guessing you have had many conversations with students (and parents too) about the benefits of a university degree; what is the lure of taking that big leap forward to the next level of learning? It is fair to say that the draw for many postgraduate students will be the tempting prospect of making themselves a more attractive proposition to graduate recruiters. While this is also likely to be an influence for undergraduates, there may well be a range of other factors in play for this group of students (e.g., see Balloo et al., 2017).[1]

Evidence suggests that general encounters with early years compulsory education will impact student aspirations and general expectations that are formed about future directions and life outcomes including the decisions made after compulsory education is complete. For example, experiences of early years primary education can influence choices made in secondary education (e.g., subject choices, the level of commitment and dedication to study) which, in turn, can also influence future pathways, including the choice of continuing to higher education (DeWitt and Archer, 2015).

Yet, when compared to their postgraduate counterparts, most undergraduate students opting to go into higher education will do so from a position of relative inexperience, with many decisions being made while the students are still almost a year away from completing their secondary education. From my experience of speaking to students at program open days and later as my personal tutees, there are many undergraduate students who choose university because they believe that alternative options are limited. There is a point when the end of high school or college is looming and a stark reality begins to hit home about 'what else am I going to do if I don't go to university?' Appropriately, many of us have laid the foundations with our young folk regarding the need for a good education if they want to equip themselves with the tools to get on in life, and, later, that a university degree is a way of developing essential skills for the jobs market; for specific pathways such as a career in medicine it is truly essential.

Even so, while this may be a primary persuader, do not underestimate the role of peer pressure. If a student's friends are all intending to head off to university and are feeling enthused about their choice of direction, the student's world may seem much smaller if intending to travel down a different route. After a lengthy period of continuous education that has subsumed almost all their formative years, a world outside of this bubble can seem scary, particularly if starting out on that new journey on their own.

Correspondingly, while peer pressure can be influential, parent pressure is often more so[2] and may be another decisive factor for a student electing to go down the higher education route (Vryonides and Gouvias, 2012). For me, this became evident from the many university open days I attended and experienced during my time as a Year 1 personal tutor. Parent power can have a considerable influence over the important decisions that need to be made. While I am sure they have the best of intentions at heart for their charge, parents too can be overly influenced by the notion that going to university seems like the best option for their son or daughter.

Finally, there are those who relish the thought of continuing their studies and aspire to spend more time in education after completing their secondary component. While this is a feasible proposition to make about those who choose to transition into postgraduate education, I suspect this may not be the number one reason why students choose to become undergraduates and so, for most, it is likely to bear much less influence when compared to the other reasons I highlight above. You should expect that the final decision will be influenced by a combination of the above factors (and others besides), although one factor may be more predominant.

I am expecting a question here about why does this matter to you as an educator with either a course or program to design? Well, the elementary answer is that the student's motivation is going to play a key role in how they will engage with the learning process once they reach the university and begin their program of study – in other words, when you meet them for the first time in the classroom. Having all this information to hand might help to explain why they all look as startled as a group of rabbits caught in a set of car headlights!

2.1.1   OK, So What Do I Study?

Once the prospective student has been tempted into life at university, there are more decisions to be made. These decisions will be just as important as that first step and will also become critical factors in determining their levels of engagement once they start their program of study.

At this early stage, one of the key questions may be, 'what do I want to study?' I was Program Director for BA Business Management at Leeds University for five years and have now worked on the program in various capacities for over ten years. In part, the diverse nature of the program attracts a lot of students who have not yet got a clear sense about what they want to do when they graduate. Without overly committing to a particular discipline, they can see that a varied program, such as Business Management, will introduce them to different aspects of the business world. I am sure the program's diversity also appeals to many parents who may know their offspring better than anyone and can see they are not ready for a commitment to a more targeted business-related specialism, such as accounting or human resource management. A compromise is often the reason students from other disciplines outside the auspices of the Business School choose to take a joint honors degree with a business subject included (Business & Modern Language; Enterprise & Music; etc.).[3]

Conversely, postgraduate students often know what program they wish to pursue from the outset and will look at which universities offer their program choice and then weigh up their options. At postgraduate level, the diversity of a broad discipline degree, such as Business Management, will offer the student who has completed a first degree in a more specialized subject discipline the opportunity to extend their commercial awareness and broaden their appeal among potential employers.

For a small minority of students, once they have started their degree program it will become apparent either that they have chosen the wrong discipline to study at degree level or, in an even smaller number of cases, that university is currently not a suitable route for them. For undergraduates, if this is going to happen, it is usually the case that it will become apparent in the first year of study, often by the end of the first term or semester. This matters if you are a program director, because attrition rates are usually scrutinized by the school or faculty and may also be a concern at institutional level. Ideally, in addition to making sure robust support measures are in place to help transition the student through induction, there needs to be a conscious effort to work with internal stakeholders such as marketing and admissions to develop mechanisms that help avoid attrition and try to resolve the issue as far as possible at the point of student recruitment.

2.2   FIRST DAY! EXPECTATIONS AND THE REALITY OF DREAMS

If you do not remember what the first day at a new school was like, then perhaps you might recall a more recent similar experience, such as starting a new job. Undoubtedly, there were several different emotions spinning round in your mind, too many for me to try and summon them all up here. So, let me see if I can pinpoint some commonalities that capture the essence of how you felt on that special day.

There are those students who head out on the first day of induction and reach the end of the day feeling enthused, confident about their direction of travel and what they need to do over the coming week or so. They are likely to have met with peers, some of whom they will be sharing their experiences with over time. They feel they can easily connect with them and their university social life is already beginning to take off. If in that group, then it is as good as it gets, and they can go home to bed and get a good night's sleep before rising the next day looking forward to embracing Day 2 of induction.

Then there is the group who feel a bit confused about what is expected of them in their new role. They may also find that the peer group they were drawn to on Day 1 also seem confused and, if honest, a little bewildered by all the information they are expected to take on board. This group of people are starting to understand what leaving home and beginning a new term of independent learning and self-responsibility is all about. While students in this group remain confident it will all work out eventually, they are beginning to feel there will be some pain to experience in the short-to-medium term while they find their feet.

The third group (and while I realize there will be umpteen more deviations within each of these three groups, I am not going to dwell on these here) consists of those who will end the first day with an impression that they could have made a dreadful mistake coming to university and just want to pack their bags at the end of the day and head off back home into the arms of someone who will be able to console them about their newfound burdens and responsibilities. They are even beginning to feel that Mr. Gibbons, the math teacher, was not such a bad sort after all, and how they wish they could walk back through their old school gates! No matter where they look, this group of students feel that every one of their peers around them seem to 'get it,' leaving them feeling isolated and lonely while everyone else seems to be confident, relaxed, and forming friendship groups – friendship groups that they already feel excluded from.

There are many reasons why each student will, very broadly speaking, be able to connect their experience with one of the three categories of Day 1 students I have outlined above. It may be governed simply by personality or levels of self-efficacy, or quite possibly by the student's natural inclination or disinclination toward feeling confident in new social settings. It could also be more situational and relate to the challenges of identifying with others from their ethnic group, socio-cultural group, or even socio-economic group. In postgraduate programs in particular, age differences can also make one feel isolated and conspicuous. A few years can make a real difference at that stage in life.

My experience is that most students do find their feet quickly, even those from the third group who feel Day 1 has been a disaster for them. In a small minority of cases, the student will quickly decide that it is the wrong time and wrong place for them and leave the program in the first few weeks. This is where conversations with parents, peers, and personal tutors (never underestimate the value of a good personal tutoring system) can make a difference, especially if the student just needs reassurance and can be encouraged to give the program a try and see how they feel later in the semester (e.g., see Pather and Dorasamy, 2018). This is good advice for those who can pull through and develop the friendship groups I allude to above. But if it really is not the right time and place then anyone who is aiming to reassure the student may be left trying to push the boulder up the hill.

Why is this so important to you as a tutor? In my experience the first few weeks are critical for the students and have an important influence on forming the sense of identity they will need to see them through the first year of their program. In a similar vein to those entering the workplace, being able to form a social identity is critical if attitudes such as engagement and commitment are to be encouraged (Thomas et al., 2021). This will become important to you as the course leader as you try to understand the temperament of the students you are teaching on your course. It is simplistic to conclude that students are not engaging with your course because they have a problem with either your teaching methods, teaching style, or the course content. This is an easy assumption to make, particularly for the teacher who is conscientious, but it is quite possibly inaccurate and may demonstrate a potential problem with your own levels of confidence. The reason the student is not engaging and lacks commitment to your course is, in truth, much more complex. Check it out. I will wager that many of these students will also have a problem with attendance in other courses on the wider program. In other words, many of them will be serial non-attenders.

2.2.1   Student Expectations

An expectation of students coming to university is that they will need to grapple with a way of working known as 'independent learning', to this point in their journey something that remains an untested concept. As we all know, moving from concept to reality can be an interesting transition and, once again, it is helpful to draw on your own experiences of starting a job with a new organization. You can visit the premises, mingle with some of the staff you will be working with, listen to stories of those who may have worked for the organization in the past, and even scour the pages of their website and scan through corporate reports and mission statements to try and prep yourself for the big day. Isn't this what you did before you started the journey of recruitment and selection for that new job you were successfully appointed to? However, any of us who have been down that route will be perfectly aware that bridging the gap between expectations and reality can entail a steep learning curve!

Again, you may ask the question, why is this important? Well, if you are tutoring students who are new to the ways of working at university, then you may encounter some resistance or, in the worst cases, reach a potential impasse between your expectations about student ownership of their own work and their expectations on this matter. This will need to be managed because it could impact on the quality of the working relationship you have with your students. Whereas most postgraduate students in study and undergraduate students who have progressed beyond the first year of their program have at least some points of reference to compare their current lot to, the only perceptions Year 1 undergraduate students will have formed come from their time in secondary-level education and a vision they have developed from listening to well-meaning others. Where expectation comes crashing into reality, the experience can be painful for both student and tutor alike.

2.3   WHAT DO I AIM TO ACHIEVE?

In this section I want to illustrate what a typical student will set out to achieve on their university journey. I have so far acknowledged some of the reasons underpinning why a student would make the all-important decision to choose your institution and your program. This takes into consideration the motivations of the student and attempts to convey some understanding about their psyche at this critical time. In the last section we reviewed some of their expectations when they arrived on the scene and now I want to consider their ambitions over the longer term or what they aspire to achieve during their time on the program. I will build on these core aims and identify other opportunities educators can offer the student to help them maximize their learning and equip themselves with the skills they need for life beyond university. How we design our courses and programs is fundamental to the overall student experience and central to enabling students to fulfill their ambitions during their time on the program. In Part II of the book I will move on to discuss the practicalities of how you can build the identified opportunities to maximize learning into your course, but for now the emphasis in Part I is all on context, that is, setting out the students' expectations, psyche, motivations, and ambitions.

So, let us imagine the scene. All those students who have just arrived on your course or program are sitting in class eagerly anticipating your first words and waiting expectantly to learn more about your offering over the next few weeks or months. As one of your students, the title and course outline sound intriguing, and so now I want to know more about the content, the delivery structure, the summative assessment, and, importantly, the formative assessment plus other opportunities for feedback and support if I need it. Beyond the practicalities (although let us not underestimate their importance) I want to know a bit more about you, the course leader, how approachable you seem, how knowledgeable you are about your subject, and how motivated you are about teaching me your subject. In other words, will you inspire me? How does all of this align with my broader aims when deciding to come to university and when I chose this program of study? Postgraduate students may already be asking the question, how does this course connect with my career plans when I graduate?

While there may be some alignment between an undergraduate's choice of program and a preferred early career path, the student's limited experience of the graduate work environment makes it harder for them to form this connection with any surety. True, there are many subjects that can be easily aligned to a more specific career choice, such as a those in medical and health-related areas or specialisms in engineering and the physical sciences. But subjects are often chosen based on interest (e.g., music, fine art, history) or because a student has performed particularly well in the subject during their previous level of study (e.g., a language, sociology, psychology, politics). This indicates that undergraduate students enrolling on these programs will not necessarily have a particular career path in mind. Indeed, it will often be the case that they have chosen their subject because of their interest or strength in it rather than because they have set out with a ten-year plan.

Here, I can draw on Business Management, the degree that I teach, as a good example of where students are attracted toward the program by the diversity of business subjects it offers. Although many new students I have spoken to over the years have not had a clear sense of what early career path they wish to pursue, there is an opportunity to connect with a broad range of business-related subjects that the student hopes will help them to identify their interests and strengths for any potential graduate careers.

Why is this important? Well, at whatever level the student is studying, if they have already formed an identity with the subject area, it will encourage the cultivation of important attitudes, such as student engagement and commitment, something you would expect if the student's degree program aligned with a particular career ambition they already have in mind. Once again, this will help the student recognize the purpose of the journey they are about to embark on and provide a connection with their long-term goals.

As I have already highlighted, while career trajectory or employability is not the only student objective of embarking on a program at either postgraduate or undergraduate level, it is often a key aspiration even though a more nuanced approach to career direction may yet need to be determined. The theoretical lens of human capital theory (Schultz, 1961) has previously been applied in this context (for examples see Donald et al., 2017; Luthans et al., 2015; Jæger,

2011) and it will be practical to draw on this theory here to try and help us identify not only the aspirations of the student but also how these could be met.

2.4   HUMAN CAPITAL THEORY

Human capital theory (Schultz, 1961) offers a rational model supporting the view that individuals will try to maximize outputs from the investments they make. Applied to the context of pedagogical learning, it examines how outcomes from education and learning are addressed within the labor market. Investments are committed by individuals in the form of an economic commitment, time devoted, and other opportunity costs they believe will endow them with core skills that are targeted by employers. These core skills become their capital and offer them a form of reward for their investments.

Human capital theory has been recognized as a framework consisting of various capital components including social, cultural, inner-value (or psychological), scholastic, and market-value capital. Each of these will be considered in turn in relation to how they can help inform the offer made by universities to students and, reciprocally, what students seek to gain from their investments. This builds on the discussion in Section 2.2 above about student expectations and what they believe is included in their psychological contract with the university.[4] Let us now take a closer look at human capital theory and how it may help inform the design of your course content and delivery with a view to meeting the ongoing development needs of your students.

Donald et al. (2017) provide a helpful account of human capital theory and how its constituent parts can contribute to our understanding of the skills students need to cultivate for their onward journey. The components of human capital they recognize as most conducive toward skills development are 1) social capital, 2) cultural capital, 3) scholastic capital, 4) inner-value capital, or psychological capital as it has also been referred to, 5) market-value capital, 6) and, finally, the skills themselves, recognized as a central element of human capital in the context of employability (Donald et al., 2017). Each component is presented in Table 2.1, along with a brief description.

When building either a program or course it will be helpful to bear in mind each constituent part of the theory. As a course leader you need to decide how you want to contribute to your students' development. If you are a program director, you can draw from the framework to ensure your program team is incorporating a balanced blend of skills and maximizing skills development across the range of courses offered on your program.

Naturally, it would be impractical for course leaders to try and incorporate every component of the framework in a single course, but being aware of what works well (e.g., how to align these skills with the intended learning outcomes and course content) is what you should be aiming for. Working with the

Table 2.1   *Aligning human capital theory with skill building at*
                university

Component	Definition
Social capital	A student's social network of contacts that they have been able to accumulate over time (this might include contacts who have influence in organizations, contacts developed through group memberships, past school friends and their families, own family members, career advisors, etc.). In the context of being a university student they would want to consider how useful these contacts are in relation to openings within graduate employment.
Cultural capital	Understanding how different cultures behave and prioritize values. Being tolerant toward a range of cultures that might behave differently to one's own. It has been noted that a strong cultural awareness is good for enhancing a student's social mobility.
Scholastic capital	The value of pre-university and university education and the self-perceived value of the grades achieved on influencing graduate employability.
Inner-value capital	The belief in one's self. The level of confidence, self-esteem, self-efficacy, and resilience to life's challenges. At university, a lot depends on a student's awareness of inner value and the support available to help develop this.
Market-value capital	Readiness for the workplace, including the skills that are of value to a graduate employer. Degrees that offer some form of work-integrated learning, including internships to gain professional experience, are particularly helpful for students to develop their market-value capital.
Skills	Recognized as the central component of human capital to employability.

Source: Adapted from Donald et al. (2017, pp. 600–601).

program director to align the skills cultivated on your course with those being developed on other courses and being able to distinguish your contribution within the wider program matters in relation to the effectiveness of the overall program. A balanced scorecard approach to the skills being developed should ensure each course is making a valuable contribution, both synthesizing and building on skills developed earlier in the program. This will also be valuable for program directors, who will want to ensure that every level of their program incorporates opportunities for students to engage with each component of the framework and that students are able to develop a rounded skill set that is relevant to the program being studied. While it is acknowledged that extra-curricular opportunities, such as work-integrated learning (e.g., short- and longer-term internships), are essential for promoting the development and refinement of employability skills, there is an important place for classroom learning when providing the scaffolding and preparatory skills in readiness for the workplace (Jackson, 2015).

Let us look at the five constituent parts of human capital theory in relation to the higher education context and then you can consider how your own course content and/or methods of delivery could incorporate at least some of these. For now, I will leave skills, the sixth component, until I discuss these in more detail in Chapter 5 of the book. By way of a reminder, the other five constituent parts that I do intend to briefly touch on here are social capital, cultural capital, scholastic capital, inner-value (or psychological) capital, and market-value capital, outline definitions of these being presented in Table 2.1.

Social capital: In more recent times, there has been talk about leveling up society and supporting those with less access to vital resources to move at least one step closer to those with abundant access. In an egalitarian society this would be a key aspiration, but as many of us live in a meritocracy, without significant intervention from government, this is less likely to happen. Within the realms of higher education, social capital refers to the network of contacts students have established, for example through their parents or other family members, group memberships, friends at university, and friends and contacts from their time in school. As a course leader your contribution to enhancing student social capital could include inviting guest speakers to come and deliver one or more of your lectures or arranging for practitioners or other experts within your subject field to support the delivery of a workshop or seminar.

I have found that industry speakers are also usually open to sharing their contact details for follow-up queries or, even better, for joining up with them on social media, such as on LinkedIn. This provides a way of helping your students to network and develop their external contacts. After all, one important lead can develop into another. It can also be helpful when students need to gain access to company information, allowing data collection from employees in relation to their own or others' organizations (e.g., to support final-year dissertations). Inviting industry speakers to contribute to your course could open up other opportunities, for example when students are seeking long-term internships or perhaps searching for graduate-level employment at the end of their degree program.

Cultural capital: By increasing a student's cultural capital you will help improve their understanding of and tolerance for other groups outside of their own immediate sphere of influence. Understanding how different cultures behave and prioritize certain values is important, as is your students having more tolerance toward other cultural groups. Tholen (2014) and Fuller et al. (2011) have noted that both social and cultural capital are key factors in relation to making students more employable (increased employability skills) and, importantly, for enhancing social mobility. Students who are well traveled will already have had the chance to increase their cultural capital, but those who are not can benefit from partner exchanges with overseas universities, whether this is for a few weeks over summer or a full academic year studying abroad.

Scholastic capital: Scholastic capital concerns the quality and value of the student's pre-university education. While there is a view that university can be a great leveler, and I have seen this materialize myself, it is often the case that those who have had to battle against the odds before they arrive at university are better prepared for the experience that awaits them. Coping with the pressures of university life is important, but it is highly likely that those taking up your course will have developed some degree of scholastic capital, though this may vary greatly. Some will be more fine-tuned toward your subject than others and this may influence the ease with which they settle into your course and the wider program.

Some employers would rather there was less emphasis on scholastic capital when honing graduates for the labor market, and more focus on other factors, including social and cultural capital, and skills development more generally. While there is a relevant argument to be presented here, a carefully designed course can incorporate the level of scholastic content that is deemed appropriate for a program of higher education so that it runs in tandem with and complements other forms of human capital referred to in this section.

Inner-value capital: According to Kaur and Sandhu (2016), as well as Luthans et al. (2004), inner-value capital, often referred to as psychological capital, is all about 'who you are.' For our purposes, we should consider this as one's self-esteem, self-efficacy, self-confidence, and sense of self-awareness.[5] We should also add optimism, hope, and resilience to the characteristics more typical of students who possess a high level of inner-value capital. So, as educators, we need to be asking ourselves questions about how we can raise the level of inner-value capital for those students who are experiencing low levels of confidence and self-esteem. At program level, personal tutors will usually be the members of the program team who get to know their charges better than most and are therefore better placed to detect issues with student confidence. Such issues could arise for a range of reasons relating to either their life at university or outside. Program directors can ensure that the personal tutoring system is working effectively on their programs, keeping in close contact with their personal tutors and heads of year to make sure there is an integrated process of support for the student.

While course leaders cannot and should not be expected to work so closely with their students that they are required to micro-manage issues external to their own course, there should be a series of checks and balances incorporated into course delivery to identify struggling students. Building in feedback mechanisms so students can identify their own strengths and weaknesses, and taking the opportunity to translate this into feedforward to ensure better performance in the future, means targeted and effective formative and summative assessment designs. A course leader offering student support hours should be a standard requirement, but as educators we also need to make sure that we make the effort to appear open and approachable to students so that they can make the most of the student support hours on offer.

Market-value capital: This is the form of human capital that is most valued by employers and refers to a person's level of readiness for the workplace. In relation to graduate careers, it pays reference to professional experience. In 2012, an extensive review of UK higher education recommended that undergraduates are offered opportunities to participate in some form of work-integrated learning alongside their degree program (Wilson Review, 2012). Such opportunities of fixed-term duration provide an excellent chance for students to gain workplace experience and either begin to develop or further hone the skills that employers wish to see in the graduate employment market. Work-integrated learning opportunities also help students make sense of their studies and can therefore complement the scholastic capital a student will develop in higher education, providing them with the necessary vision to integrate theory and practice. Even so, course leaders need to work smart and embed opportunities to engage with practice in the design of their own courses. Incorporating examples of practice into course content and delivery can be a simple matter (e.g., incorporating problem-solving and/or research exercises with real-life or fictitious cases; inviting practitioners to teach on the course).

In Part II of the book I will be providing a stepped outline of how you can plan and design your course. While I have only briefly alluded to skills in this chapter, these will form part of a much more detailed discussion in Chapter 5 when I will also offer a framework to identify the type of skills that we need to build into our courses and programs at university. More generally, several of the elements of human capital development referred to above can be enhanced and incorporated into course delivery by integrating them as skills development activities in your teaching sessions. Again, this is very straightforward to do but will offer students an opportunity to engage with and practice developing a range of skills, particularly those students at undergraduate level who will have little experience of the workplace. I will talk more about how these skills can be included in course design in Part II of the book.

2.5   SUMMARY

My central aim in this chapter has been to help raise awareness of a student's journey up to the point where they arrive at university and are prepared to start their program. Understanding the student's journey thus far and their potential mindset as they embark on their year ahead will help you when planning and preparing the delivery of your course, particularly over the first few sessions.

In the remaining three chapters of Part I, I will outline links between course design and what I characterize as the central pillars of student development: student confidence (Chapter 3), student engagement (Chapter 4), and skills development (Chapter 5). I begin in the next chapter by starting a conversation about the critically important subject of student confidence: what you can do to help them develop self-efficacy and overcome the barriers arising from a fear of failure. I discuss the need for us to work on being more inclusive in our teaching practice to ensure groups and individuals alike are not left feeling sidelined. When facing up to any students who are giving you reason for concern, you must keep reminding yourself that there is always an underlying reason for their behavior. Being aware of the journey they will have been on, including the challenges they may have encountered along the way, as well as taking into consideration the hurdles that are yet to come, will hopefully help you when designing and delivering your course.

NOTES

1. While improved career prospects were recognized as the main influence, other strong influences included personal development, to enhance quality of life, to improve potential future earnings, for the enjoyment of learning, to change direction in life, and to make friends.
2. Parent pressure can also be adversarial.
3. Doing so can offer the student the best of both worlds. They can take their passion, interest, or hobby to the next level while also gaining exposure to a business-related course that will have more general appeal to a wider range of employers when the student graduates.
4. While the psychological contract is normally referred to within the realms of the employment relationship and represents the unwritten agreement of expectations that exist between employer and employee, I am drawing on its principles here to analogize within the context of the student and university relationship.
5. I discuss these in more detail in Chapter 3.

3. Developing student confidence

I referred to student confidence in Chapter 2 when discussing the inner-value component of human capital theory. More generally, there are a multiplicity of reasons why levels of confidence may radically differ between students. More specifically, levels of confidence may be dependent on the student's readiness to undertake a particular activity or task and the skills that are required to accomplish it.

While feelings of uncertainty can have an impact on levels of student confidence when they arrive at university, the intention is that this will change as university-driven induction activities are rolled out over the first weeks before teaching begins. In many cases student apprehensions concerning the journey they are about to embark on will be negated as they meet with their peers and share experiences, finding solace in doing so. This can be a particularly challenging period for those needing to embrace a different culture and seek out potential friends with whom they can readily identify. During the induction period, the role played by academic staff, including program directors and personal tutors, is critical, and the visibility of these staff can be fundamental to the new student during this time and in the early weeks of teaching. However, where feelings of low confidence are carried by the student into the weeks where teaching begins, this is where you, the course leader, can make a notable contribution to their psyche by promoting their feelings of belonging and well-being, and, of course, a sense of value as they begin to realize that their contribution matters.

There are some easy quick wins to be had as you begin your course in the first week or two. While it is more of a challenge to recognize individual students in large lectures, where a substantial number of people will be in attendance, you will hopefully have incorporated a mix of smaller, more intimate settings, such as seminar groups or workshops. In a seminar consisting of 30 students or fewer, it is easy to scan the room, allowing you to 'see' and get to know everyone. This is an ideal situation for me because it allows me to distinguish between students who are engaging in the class and those who are less assertive in their behavior.

In a larger group of 50–60 students upwards it is not so straightforward to be aware of student behavior and body language, particularly if you are only together for a short session each week or fortnight. If you can arrange a teaching assistant[1] to support you during these larger interactive sessions then you can operate the class between you when the students are working on a task. This way, you can both work your way round the tables and spend some time with each group. Doing so helps you both get to know the students, and they will value your contribution and interest in them. You can also help reduce any uncertainties the students may have about the task they are being asked to perform and address more general questions about the course that they would otherwise feel reluctant to raise in front of the larger group.

A confident student who feels they are in control of their situation will be much more likely to engage with your course and feel ready to learn. As I briefly discussed in Chapter 2, students who are low in confidence from the outset are starting out in a bad place where they will quite possibly find the transition to higher education a more traumatic, stressful, and potentially lonely experience. No matter how many times they have been told that their new learning environment will mean a step up in relation to autonomy, responsibility, and self-regulation, it is only now that it is hitting home just what this means. The impact on the student of feeling lost and having little sense of control can, unsurprisingly, lead to poor academic performance and an increased likelihood of dropping out altogether (Gillock and Reyes, 1999; Murtaugh et al., 1999). If you are a program director and responsible for attrition rates, your faculty seniors may be watching closely! Let us have a look at some of the problems with student confidence and how to overcome this barrier to learning in student pedagogy.

3.1 BUILDING SELF-EFFICACY

According to Bandura (1997), effort you will expend pursuing an activity, your persistence pursuing the activity, the resilience to adverse events while pursuing the activity, and even choosing to chase that activity in the first place, will be influenced by your general level of self-efficacy. Self-efficacy, which relates to an individual's beliefs about their ability to perform an action, should not be confused with self-esteem, which is more about the individual's overall sense of worthiness. I will discuss self-esteem later in Chapter 3 along with its relationship with a fear of failure.

Bandura recognized the significance of evaluating an experience through the process of self-reflection with a view to influencing a change in both how the experience is perceived and, subsequently, the behavior. In situations where people experience low self-efficacy, they will often perceive events as being more difficult than they are (glass half empty). This tends to mean they will exert low effort or give up entirely, leading to more stress and exacerbating those feelings of low self-belief. In comparison, those who experience high self-efficacy will, typically, see difficult situations as a challenge they can rise to and shrug off any issues of doubt (glass half full). You will have guessed that those in this situation are more likely to be successful in the task outcomes and therefore reconfirm their decision to back themselves, expounding their feelings of high self-belief and, subsequently, increasing their likelihood of accomplishing the end goal. Bandura states that merely developing the requisite skills and knowledge is not sufficient to accomplish the end goal but needs to be accompanied by self-efficacy. Therefore, self-efficacy is a key factor when developing human agency.

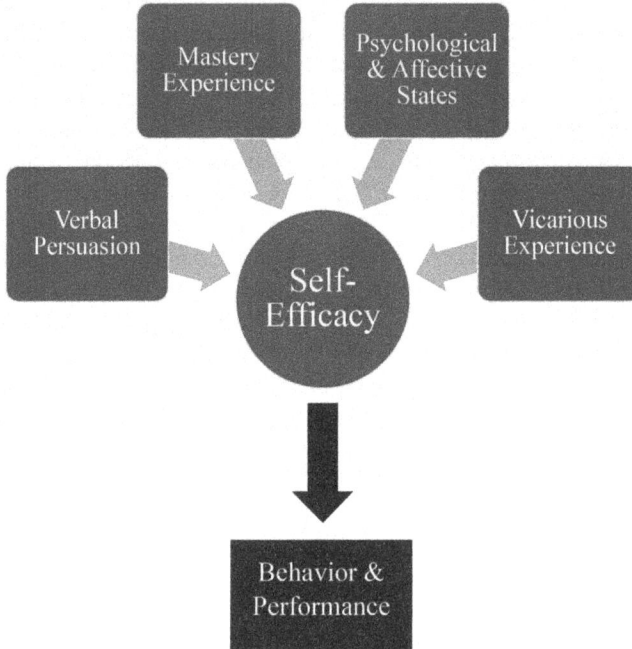

Source: Inspired by Bandura (1997).

Figure 3.1   Developing self-efficacy

In his conceptual framework (see the example presented in Figure 3.1), Bandura (1997) stresses that self-efficacy will be influenced by four central pillars consisting of verbal persuasion, psychological and affective states, mastery experience, and vicarious experience. Let us have a look at what this means.

Verbal persuasion: When someone we regard highly (perhaps someone we identify as a role model) convinces us we can achieve an objective, this helps to boost our self-belief and it is likely we will exert more effort in attempting to achieve the said objective. Having someone we regard as a role model who can leave a positive influence on us during our formative years is often the origin of our self-belief. Feedback when attempting to complete a task is important here as well, with positive or encouraging feedback stimulating our self-efficacy beliefs and negative feedback more likely to decrease our levels of self-efficacy.

Psychological and affective states: Mental health and well-being will impact the development of our self-efficacy beliefs. For example, if we experience a low mood or longer-term suffering from anxiety or depression, then this may also influence our self-belief when trying to accomplish a task. Even a simple day-to-day task can seem onerous and challenging when our mental health and well-being has taken a battering. The emotion we experience when undertaking the task will also impact our psychological state, synchronously leading to either increased self-efficacy (e.g., feelings of satisfaction or enjoyment from undertaking the task) or reduced feelings of self-efficacy (e.g., if we experience extreme fatigue or if the task leads us to states of anxiety or negative stress).

Mastery experience: Being successful in a new challenge can help us to gain mastery experience, which may be due to the hours of practice we dedicate to learning the skill or to developing the requisite knowledge. However, the benefit from knowing we have previously risen to the challenge and already accomplished the task will help us to develop an expertise (e.g., understanding the best way of managing the process or procedures; becoming more effective and/or efficient in our behavior when accomplishing the task). Of course, the adverse may be true where we have failed to accomplish the task in the past, although learning from past mistakes can also help us to grow and become more accomplished in future. Bandura recognized this as the most influential source of self-efficacy.

Vicarious experience: Improving self-efficacy via vicarious experience (observing others successfully accomplishing a task) relies once again on our encounters with a positive role model. The power of the vicarious learning process is influenced by the observed actions and behaviors of someone we identify with as a positive role model when they are performing either the same or a similar task. The power and influence of this person is a key factor here and may well be associated with how closely we identify with them. Examples of a role model could include a mentor, teacher, coach, or family member.

So, what does this mean for the self-efficacy of students enrolled on your course or program? Well, it is evident that self-efficacy is a vital ingredient of the student's ability to achieve. Drawing on Bandura's conceptual framework helps to give us a level of granularity to better understand self-efficacy and to generate practical ideas about how we can plan and deliver our courses to support students in this way. I revisit confidence and self-efficacy in Part II of the book when looking at developing a toolkit for course design.

Next, I want to discuss the critical issue of student mindset and its inextricable relationship with self-efficacy.

3.1.1   Academic Self-Efficacy and Mindset

Self-efficacy is recognized as a state of mind that is not static or fixed and can be situationally dependent. We must realize that a student's aptitude toward academic self-efficacy (i.e., how confident a student will be about their own academic abilities) is, in part, going to be shaped by the educators and others of influence that the student will meet during their time at university. This emphasizes the central role educators play in the student's academic development, being equipped with the means to coax out the best from the student, enabling them to perform at their optimum level. From the discussion so far, it is evident that while one of our primary functions as educators is to provide the student with the opportunities to learn new skills, this will need to operate in tandem with a focus on building and maintaining their levels of self-efficacy – a state of mind that is both fluid and situationally dependent.

Beatson et al. (2019) emphasize the need to consider a person's mindset when understanding their level of self-efficacy. In connection with learning, mindset research identifies both a fixed mindset (i.e., whatever I do I cannot change my proficiency in this task – the activity/task cannot be learned) and a growth mindset (i.e., the firm belief that one can build, adapt, and learn new skills and abilities and improve at a particular task – the activity/task can be learned). Typically, students of the latter disposition are focused on improvement, growth, and progression.

However, dividing students into this binary categorization of fixed or growth mindsets is not always helpful. As I have mentioned, mindset is not static and so anyone demonstrating a fixed mindset can be encouraged toward developing a more malleable or growth mindset that connects learning with the vision of personal development. Tutors therefore need to be actively guiding their student cohorts toward a growth mindset if they wish to encourage better engagement and a good learning environment. Many studies have shown that fixed mindsets can be shifted toward growth mindsets by employing educational interventions (e.g., Dweck, 2017; Rissanen et al., 2016).

Students with a growth mindset are much more likely to seek support for their learning from academic tutors, personal tutors, and other teaching staff, and even through having discussions and working collegiately and collaboratively with their peers. We must never underestimate the value of students seeking out learning support from their peers while also acting as help providers for other students. Students who are high in self-efficacy and believe that learning is something malleable are more likely to offer themselves as help givers within those peer support networks (Zander et al., 2018). Forming their own support networks either during in-class teaching or outside within other forums (e.g., small study groups working together in preparation for an exam or other forms of assessment) can be critical for some students who find that the proximity and intimacy of those friendship groups is helpful for sensemaking, sharing learning strategies, and confirming their understanding of content.

This also raises the need for course tutors to recognize the importance of small-group learning, typically demonstrated through the seminar or workshop environment. As educators we must be aware of the necessity to create opportunities for students to become integrated in academic and social support networks on a regular and sustained basis when working together in these situations. Others have highlighted the effectiveness of learning being extended through both in-class and external social networks and that peer learning and peer tutoring is an effective way of developing a range of academic skills, beside promoting student integration and participation (e.g., see Lueg et al., 2016; Parker et al., 2016).

As educators we should be well placed to help initiate and support the maintenance of student peer groups and networks by promoting collaboration in class and through group assessment methods. Developing a collegiate way of working and promoting peer interaction as a form of social learning can also help students adapt their own learning styles by seeing what works well for others and adopting positive behaviors they see demonstrated by their peers. We can promote the activity by organizing group work in our live interactive teaching sessions, such as seminars and workshops, and, for example, where group work has been designed for either the formative or summative course assessment. This allows students time to work and interact with their group members on their projects while also giving them some autonomy in these sessions, which may also encourage better attendance. In doing so you will aid the development of student peer support networks while promoting an opportunity for those who wish to take a lead in supporting peer learning in their group. Environments such as these that allow students to learn from tutors and peers alike also offer them an invaluable source of feedback on their ideas and methods of working that they can put into practice and trial in a safe environment that is not going to be too critical or judgmental.

Acquiring a growth mindset also matters when it comes to resilience and the extent to which a student will persist in the advent of inferior performance or even failure. Students with a growth mindset are more likely to decide to refocus their efforts and make sure they perform better next time. They are confident they will change, adapt, and learn over time, increasing their chances of success at a given task. For these students, a low mark means they need to adapt their preparation strategies for next time rather than accepting it is an indication of their intelligence or general levels of ability. Conversely, those students with a fixed mindset, who believe change cannot happen, are more likely to crumble when challenged with inferior performance or failure. It has also been proposed that these students are less likely to seek out and use feedback and more likely to place the blame for their failure or low performance elsewhere (Dweck, 2014). For example, in an educational setting, rather than look to themselves to provide answers as to why they underperformed, they may choose to blame the quality of the teaching or support they received while the course was being delivered.

Be aware that an individual can have a mixture of a fixed and a growth mindset in relation to different tasks, activities, or even particular skills. This means that it cannot be assumed an individual will have either a fixed or growth mindset that can be consistently applied to everything. Even so, there tends to be a predominance of one over the other. Evidence suggests that the experience of higher levels of academic self-efficacy is positively related to a growth mindset (Zander et al., 2018), meaning that students who are self-efficacious toward a particular activity are much more likely to believe they can develop and learn to become proficient in that or any related task over time. This can also influence the attitudes of others, such as peers and other group members when students are working together on a task. Helping to develop self-efficacy, encouraging a growth mindset, and therefore breaking the barrier of a fixed mindset, can also have positive repercussions among the wider cohort the student is working with, a contagion that you would want to encourage!

So, you can see how critical it will be to shift the mindset of students who are demonstrating a fixed mindset (i.e., those who will resist training and learning growth because they don't believe it will benefit them) to a growth mindset, where possibilities to enhance learning and developing new learning strategies that will benefit them are embraced by the student. Moving to a growth mindset will help promote resilience, improve personal outcomes, and enhance attitudes toward learning.

3.2   HELPING TO OVERCOME THE STUDENT'S FEAR OF FAILURE

While fear is often an emotion experienced when threats are real, it also evolves from dangers that are imagined and, in truth, do not exist. Whether stemming from situations that are real or imagined, an individual's fear often arises from their perceived loss of control. Choi (2021) suggests that we, as educators, can assist students in overcoming their fear of failing, and hence improve their academic performance, by helping to create suitable learning environments. In addition to impacting academic performance, fear of failure can also affect student engagement, cause academic procrastination (i.e., using strategies to keep avoiding a task that has been set), result in poor self-regulation, and produce feelings of shame – not the types of behavior you would wish for in a student entering the realms of higher education, considering the increased levels of independence, autonomy, and self-regulation they will need to take charge of their own learning. As educators we need to find techniques that will encourage those students who suffer from fear of failure to 'unlearn' their existing behaviors and dispel the emotion of fear. Let us take a closer look at this phenomenon.

3.2.1 Reasons Why a Fear of Failure Exists

In academic settings, fear of failure has been associated with feelings of shame, test anxiety, and the need to achieve (often associated with the high bar some students set). As mentioned, it can be a cause of an 'avoidance to learn' disposition or, at least, procrastination toward learning or beginning a particular task (e.g., starting an assignment). One particularly good example that springs to mind from my own experience is the small number of students who, each year, decide to avoid starting their dissertation and convince themselves that there is other work they must prioritize, moving the inevitable start date back a few weeks. Of course, this becomes mission creep, and they convince themselves with one excuse after another to push the start date even further back until, in some cases, far too little time is afforded to undertaking a much bigger piece of work than the student envisaged. Of course, in some of these cases, the decision to avoid starting their dissertation 'just yet' is because an anxiety exists about the fear of failure.

Neuroscience would have us believe that fear is a conditioned response to a stimulus situation, such as a classroom environment, the presence of a tutor in the classroom environment, or the presence of fellow students. If we are to tempt our students out of their apparent reticence to engage in classroom debate and discussion then it is important that we, as educators, can look round a room and immediately spot that some students look eager and ready for the challenge of the next hour or so while others are gazing at their phones, or down at the desk in front of them. Do not despair. All is not lost. These students have at least made the effort to attend today's class. Worse still are those who have not made any effort at all to attend. At least we can rise to the challenge of enthusing and engaging those in the room, whereas those who are elsewhere are more of a challenge given they are beyond our immediate reach.

The conditioned response I refer to above could originate from a past classroom experience or even a range of experiences where the student has grown wary of making any contribution in case it is evaluated in a negative way by their peers. It is possible that this form of evaluation apprehension could result in no contribution until you, and others in the class, can tempt the student out of their silence. For this to happen the student will need to build rapport and

Table 3.1   Student fear of failure in an educational setting

A fear of failure can lead to:	
Performance avoidance	an inclination to avoid events identified as either uncertain or unfavorable (procrastination; task avoidance strategy)
Learned helplessness	experiencing either low or no control over events; giving up attempting to achieve a task; low resilience
Self-handicapping	developing excuses for low performance to protect self-esteem rather than taking responsibility
Feelings of shame	more commonly associated with those with a high fear of failure; when an individual generalizes the failure to the entire self rather than a specific event or action

Source: Inspired by Choi (2021).

trust with not only their peers but, more importantly, their tutor. You really do have the power and influence to persuade your students to drop their old behaviors and become new converts to class discussion. This may be a painstaking exercise, but it is within your influence to do so. One of the most crucial aspects is building a supportive environment for your students. Trust is a vital ingredient of effective leadership and if your students feel they can trust you then they will learn to follow you.

Choi (2021) helps us interpret the fear of failure from a multidimensional perspective, and it is helpful to stop and consider how the underlying factors he recognizes are associated with a student's fear of failing. The outcomes from a fear of failure are presented in Table 3.1, with a more detailed account including underlying factors coming beneath.

Choi proposes that low competence expectancies and a fear of failure lead to a situation recognized as *performance avoidance*, or an inclination to avoid events identified by the individual as either uncertain or unfavorable. I have already mentioned procrastination toward beginning a task and this can be identified as a performance or task avoidance strategy. A low competence expectancy can also impact the setting of performance or achievement-oriented goals.

A fear of failure is often associated with situations where the individual will be experiencing low levels of control or even no control at all. In situations such as these, the individual has been identified as exhibiting *learned helplessness*, which encourages a person to willingly give up a particular task or even not to pursue or attempt the task at all, merely accepting failure. An example that readily springs to mind is a situation where a student feels so unprepared for an exam that they do not even bother to attend, with the result being they are marked absent. I have also experienced situations where a student attends the exam but gives up very soon after the start and leaves a few lines of an attempted answer before departing the exam arena. As an example of learned helplessness, this typifies a student who will not engage with the task because they fundamentally believe that no matter how hard they try, there can only be one outcome: abject failure. It has also been reported that learned helplessness is strongly associated with test anxiety. As you will no doubt have concluded, this links seamlessly with the above definition for a fixed mindset. Going back to the point raised about the significance of feeling in control, we can see that increasing the level of control in a situation may lead to a reduction in setback pressure and feelings of failure experienced by a student.

I am sure we have all made excuses in the past for substandard performance, and if the expectation is to fail or perform badly then we may adopt something known as *self-handicapping*. A fear of failure can lead to self-handicapping, a behavior whereby we try to protect our self-esteem by finding an excuse rather than taking responsibility for failing to achieve in a given situation. Self-handicapping has been defined as 'constructing impediments to per-formance to protect or enhance one's perceived competence' (Schwinger et al., 2014, p. 744). Making excuses and using these as reasons for our poor performance, or in anticipation of poor performance for a future event, is one way of self-handicapping. This could involve moving the causal attribution from poor performance due to low ability (e.g., I failed my exam because I lack competence in this subject field) to an externalization (e.g., I have been ill recently and unable to concentrate on my studies). To typify it we can say that self-handicapping is an attempt to externalize any acts (or potential acts) of failure (acts of success tend to be internalized). I guess we can all lay claim to actions of this nature at some point in our lives. Again, a fear of failure has been identified as a key antecedent of a need to self-handicap.

It has been argued that *feelings of shame* is an emotion that goes to the very heart of feelings of failure and that shame begins to emerge when the failure, or fear of failure, is attributed to a lack of ability. While the feeling of failure may be attributed to a specific action or event, there is often a tendency to feel the entire self has been left wanting and to generalize the emotion more globally to the self, hence a broader feeling of shame. McGregor and Elliot (2005) found that individuals with a higher fear of failure were more likely to experience greater feelings of shame than those with a lower fear of failure.

3.2.2 The Relationship between a Fear of Failure and Mindset

Taking each of these factors into consideration we can see how they align with the mindsets that I alluded to earlier. Shifting students from a fixed mindset to a growth mindset will help to move them away from an inclination toward each of these limiting tendencies and the fear of failure. A growth mindset encourages the student to 'have a go' without concerns about the repercussion from how they will be observed and evaluated by peers or important others – in other words, without a fear of failure. While on the subject of 'fearing failure,' let us have a closer look at the consequences of doing so.

Some educators believe that having a fear of failure is a good thing; that it can encourage learning and growth in the student. Indeed, they see it as a necessary component of the learning journey that the student will embark on. Feigenbaum (2021) recognizes student failure as belonging to one of two camps: what can be distinguished as either generative or stigmatized forms of failure. Generative failure is seen as positive in the approach to learning and something we can all resonate with along our journey through life. This is the belief that failure leads to a lesson we can learn from to help us grow and flourish in our future attempts at the same or a related task. It involves a natural process of experimentation where we can learn from the feedback – what Burger (2012) refers to as 'failing effectively.'

While failing may not always be a comfortable experience for the student, it offers an opportunity for feedback from someone more experienced, which will hopefully help the student to grow. We can immediately see the positive aspect of failing and use these experiences to learn from the feedback, whether this is self-generated (i.e., from own analysis of what did not work well) or from someone else in a position to pass on their experience and advice to help us improve the next time round. It is possible to leave the failed experience feeling positive about the outcome because it procures a sense of confidence that can be utilized as part of the overall learning experience to improve our performance next time. I am assuming you have already made the connection between this and the principles of a growth mindset discussed earlier. The student with a growth mindset sees failure as generative and is more likely to seek alternative strategies, doubling up on their efforts in preparation for next time to ensure a better performance and doing all that is possible to avoid failing again.

As you may expect, generating the perception of a positive learning experience from a situation of failure cannot be applied to all students. In its place, many will encounter what Feigenbaum refers to as 'stigmatized failure.' And so, while we need to be aware that for some students a form of generative failure can bring positivity, we also need to acknowledge that for many students failure will also carry the burden of stigma.

Figure 3.2 shows that whereas generative failure is associated with a growth mindset, stigmatized failure is associated with a fixed mindset, meaning that students who fear failure (stigmatized) are less convinced by the argument that their knowledge and skill set can be improved through engaging with the learning process. For this group of students, unless they are convinced there is a good chance they will achieve success, they have a greater tendency to see failing as making them look inferior and feel shame, meaning they will be less comfortable about undertaking the task.

Fixed mindset leads to:
• **Stigmatized failure**
• which can be both emotionally and cognitively harrowing
• a belief that both knowledge and skills set are fixed and cannot be improved through learning
• leads to fear of failure
• reduces risk taking and creativity – safety from operating within comfort zone
• generates a lower level of resilience

Growth mindset leads to:
• **Generative failure**
• failure perceived as positive to learning
• a belief that learning is fluid – one can learn, adapt, and build new skills and abilities
• one can learn to improve from feedback (self-generated or external)
• provides an opportunity to grow in confidence and improve performance
• generates a higher level of resilience

Source: Inspired by Feigenbaum (2021).

Figure 3.2   Mindset and its influence on perceived failure

Feigenbaum goes on to say that, in his experience, higher education institutions often breed the wrong kind of outcome from episodes of failure, which ends up being both emotionally and cognitively harrowing, working against any opportunity for the student to turn the experience into a positive outcome. Stigmatized failure is the true fear of failure and means that students will be less likely to operate outside of their comfort zone and hence unlikely to take risks or to be creative in the way they operate. Additionally, these students are less likely to persevere when setbacks occur (i.e., there is an impact on their resilience).

So, as educators, we need to raise the question: 'How can I try to break this cycle by tapping into the fears of the student and persuading them to move on from seeing failure as a stigma to instead seeing it as something that is more generative and opens the door to a new learning experience?' To answer this question, we need to return to the debate about fixed versus growth mindsets and how important it is to promote the latter. When a student believes that outcomes can only be attributed to their own efforts, there is an increased danger that this narrow perspective returns them repeatedly to the cry of 'oh, I tried as hard as I could and still failed. I just must face up to the fact that I am a loser and will never improve' – a typical example of how a student who is stigmatized by repeatedly failing a particular task feels.

This takes us back to the earlier conversation about self-efficacy and how the educator needs to develop interventions that can help improve the student's level of self-belief. For some students, feelings of low self-efficacy will be more of a natural disposition and so building strategies for students to develop a more positive mindset on your course may also help to support them elsewhere on their program.

In Part II of the book I will move on to investigate strategies that you can use in your teaching to help students overcome the factors that lead to a fear of failing: strategies that not only serve the purposes of your own course, but can also be built upon by the students and used for their remaining time at university.

3.3   THE IMPORTANCE OF INCLUSIVITY

I discuss inclusive practice when I move on to consider student engagement in Chapter 4. Even so, it also warrants a place in the conversation about developing student confidence. Its place here builds on some of the earlier discussion in this chapter and will help to set the scene for when, in Part II, I move on to disclose some of the strategies that can be built into our teaching.

The wealth of cultural experience and diversity we usually have at our disposal in higher education means university can be a unique opportunity for students to enhance their learning experience (e.g., emotional and cultural awareness; building cultural capital). However, to reap the benefits from pro-social activity it is important for students to quickly build their identities as they start their university journey. We, as tutors, can play our part, needing to be sensitive to both the individual differences and cultural diversity that exist in our tutor groups. By being aware of how critical inclusive practice is for all those who attend our teaching sessions, we can support students with identity building and help to mitigate the erection of any barriers that can soon emerge. In this sense, being inclusive means being aware of and more sensitive toward group differences (e.g., culture, gender), but I am also referring to individual differences – for example, students with learning impediments[2] and the additional challenges this may bring for them (including in undertaking practices that seem straightforward for many of us, such as reading and note-taking).

Where learning impediments exist, this can raise additional challenges at a time when many students will already be out of their comfort zone with the new ways of learning and working at university. For these students, and other students who feel isolated or alienated, it may be more of a challenge to form an identity with the wider group.

While it might not be feasible to monitor every student in your teaching group, it is helpful to be aware of the additional challenges to learning that these students may have to negotiate. For students who feel a sense of exclusion due to their difference or learning impediment, in the worst-case scenario this could increase absenteeism as frustrations in the classroom environment lead to a student becoming disengaged and attempting to complete the course remotely.

Past studies have found that students diagnosed with dyslexia[3] suffer from low self-esteem and elevated levels of both academic and social anxiety (Webster, 2016; Carroll and Iles, 2006). Among other challenges, note-taking and expressing ideas in writing can be a problem for this group of students. Although these challenges can be compensated for with appropriate mitigations for summative assessments, students with learning impediments are unlikely to receive the same support for formative assessment exercises or routine activities that take place in the classroom.

To some extent, the switch toward a more technology-assisted learning environment has helped to provide additional support with captioning and lecture capture meaning that lecture notes are readily provided, but this is not always so valuable where the quality of session recordings is dubious and within the seminar and workshop environment where the quality of the activity is often dependent on two-way interaction and working in small groups.

Similarly, students diagnosed with dyspraxia have also been found to have challenges with handwriting, organization, and time management. Both groups of students receive support from universities more generally in relation to additional time and consideration in summative assessment and, in some cases, having access to laptops and mentors, but the benefits may be limited during live class activities.

In Chapter 4 I discuss inclusivity and its relationship with student engagement. Also, in Part II of the book I will explain how to implement some simple additions to your weekly schedule so that your teaching can take into consideration the diversity of the student population and help you to become more inclusive in your teaching practice. In addition to improving the learning experience for your students, these changes could make a significant contribution to your cohort pass rate and avoid absences from the assessment. Moreover, if you can make all students feel appreciated and included you will see their confidence growing week by week and reduce the possibilities of absences from your taught sessions and the inevitable disengagement that will follow.

3.4   CHAPTER SUMMARY

In Chapter 3 I have once again tried to take us on a journey to understand the student's mindset and help you to recognize some of the problems that will arise around student confidence and the fear of failing. Hopefully, if you are better aware of these potential problems you will also be equipped to support the student to overcome their self-doubts, something that may be particularly challenging for a student with low resilience at the beginning of their program.

Mindset is a critical factor in all of this, and hopefully understanding the difference between a fixed and growth mindset will help you to build a foundation to work from and support each of your students to move toward the growth mindset that will be more conducive to their own potential for learning and, subsequently, the successful outcomes that they seek. Some students will be naturally inclined to have a fixed mindset, but for others this mindset may simply be related to new uncertainties inspired by the transition to university. As tutors, we can persuade a change in student mindset through careful planning of our course design.

I also discussed the all-important area of student inclusivity and the need to be aware of how and where diversity exists among student groups. Additionally, I emphasized the need to be conscious of the requirement for a more equitable approach to both our teaching delivery and our course design, aimed at encouraging and enabling all our students to get involved with class discussions and other forms of interactivity that can help them build an identity with the group.

In Chapter 4 I move on to investigate the subject of student engagement, which, based on the principle that a confident university student is much more likely to become a student that can readily engage with their work, follows on seamlessly from the topic of student confidence and mindset.

In Part II of the book I will set out the strategies that you can employ in your teaching to help instigate some of the positive changes needed to encourage confidence to shine through your students. You can incorporate these strategies into the planning when designing your course.

NOTES

1. Class sizes of above 30 students can become difficult to manage effectively and, in these cases, lone tutors should be supported by a teaching assistant. Faculties are often supportive of a need to make use of postgraduate research students to help with teaching assistant roles wherever these are deemed necessary. Not only does this help you to facilitate the classroom experience for the students you are teaching and ensure that these students are supported in their learning, but it also offers the postgraduate research student an opportunity to gain teaching experience that will be invaluable as they enter their early academic careers.
2. Some of the most common forms of learning impediments that I am referring to here include dyslexia, ADHD, dyscalculia, and dyspraxia.
3. More sophisticated diagnoses help us to recognize dyslexia as being much more prevalent among a typical group of students than some imagine.

4. Maximizing student engagement

In the last chapter we looked at how to build student confidence, a factor that is likely to have a key role in whether students readily engage with your course content. I have had many mid-term conversations with frustrated colleagues who are struggling to maintain the same level of engagement that was present at the outset of their course. It is too easy to make the basic assumption that waning engagement is due to a fault on your part. I am an optimist, and while there will always be some students who feel they would rather avoid your specially prepared classroom experience, it is not always because they do not like the content or your delivery style, even though the learning environment can also make an important contribution toward either fostering or inhibiting student engagement in learning (Lardy et al., 2022). Group dynamics are important, and members of a seminar or workshop group who are drawn together by the magnetism of your sessions will be more likely to become regular attenders.

Including checks along the way in the shape of formative assessment and feedback is something the students will appreciate because it can offer tangible evidence of their learning so far. It will offer structure to your course because it helps the students to focus on specific time points within the overall timeline of delivery. Because formative assessment is built into the course part way through its life cycle, it can be used as a tool to provide feedback to the student on their progress and becomes a method of maintaining engagement in their learning.

Providing the student with a clear vision of how both formative and summative assessment align with course content and its learning outcomes helps with sensemaking (helping to address questions such as 'why am I being asked to undertake this task?') and linking the course to wider program objectives and the student's own goals.[1] Such sensemaking helps to reduce uncertainty, which, in turn, will help to increase the student's level of engagement with your course.

So, formative assessment can help build student confidence by communicating that they are meeting their learning targets and/or by highlighting areas of content where they need to focus their learning for improvement. Additionally, the results from formative assessment exercises can help the tutor to evaluate where their class is in terms of attainment and knowledge development and whether they need to consider adjustments to their teaching delivery strategy for the remainder of the course.

In this chapter I discuss how you can encourage student engagement and hopefully allay some of the fears and self-doubts that may creep into your own teaching by highlighting the multitude of reasons why a student may seem shy and appear to be avoiding you at all costs.

4.1   FORMING IDENTITIES

Identity is a complex construct that is not only multifaceted but also fluid and never static. We adapt who we identify with and how we identify according to those we recognize as a representation of our 'most suitable' selves (Woodward, 2003).[2] Brzeski (2017) recognizes that the process of identifying with others requires active engagement and awareness and that identifying with a particular person or group is something that we consciously choose to do. We form identities in a comparable way to how we choose our in-groups (people we associate with) and out-groups (people we disassociate with). So, difference and sameness and setting boundaries around those we recognize as in-groups and identify with is important.

In an educational setting this is no different, and so it makes sense that if we want our students to identify themselves as 'in' (i.e., part of the in-group) then there needs to be some common interest between themselves and the rest of the group that they can associate with. Here, when talking about the group I am referring to the class and not the wider course or program cohort. For a student to commit to learning in a deep, analytical way, this may involve them developing a new identity with the learning group. As it is usually the case that we will have multiple identities, committing to this new identity within the classroom or wider program may bring conflicts, or opportunity costs, for the student. For example, if they are to become a diligent student who is now committed to their new environment, this may involve making life choices that require suppressing other identities they have previously formed (e.g., attending class means missing part-time work opportunities or not over-committing to university sports activities).

4.1.1   Building a Sense of Social Presence

Social presence helps to generate knowledge through the shared experience of a supportive learning environment in which students feel comfortable. It has been defined by Biocca et al. (2003) as a 'sense of being with another' (p. 456). As a result, pertinent questions might be: 'How do we build social presence and identity for our students?' and 'What does this mean in relation to our central questions in this chapter about developing and maintaining student engagement?' To build an identity with their learning group, a student will need to feel socially secure within that group. For example, students need to develop a sense of security within the group so that they can interact and make contributions to class discussions within a safe environment without a threat of alienation due to detrimental judgment or evaluation by others within the group. This involves the development of mutual trust between group members.

Knowing that a student is operating in a safe environment through the development of mutual trust with other group members becomes particularly important during small-group problem-solving activities where participation and cooperation is essential. When students feel they are part of a supportive environment in which other group members value their contribution they are much more likely to feel unencumbered in their creative thinking and decision-making. According to Jaber and Kennedy (2017), identity with a group is augmented by social interaction and so helping to build that ambiance of a secure environment within your teaching groups will encourage student contribution and, along with it, a sense of group identity. This provides a compelling argument in favor of keeping the same student teaching group composition for every seminar or workshop throughout the duration of your course.

Why does any of this matter? Well, it may be the case that the student has other drivers that motivate them to engage with the course and its content (e.g., a particular interest in the subject; enthused by your teaching style). But, in circumstances where other drivers have not yet been established, social relations can play a powerful role in the formation of student identities. It may also be the weekly gathering of faces that the student has an affinity with and encourages them to attend and engage with the class content on a regular basis. Identifying with the group could be one more reason the student engages with your course.

It can also work the other way too. If the student does not feel comfortable with other students in their class and feels a cold shiver down their spine at the thought of attending a dysfunctional session where they are likely to sit on their own and perhaps feel alienated before being asked to join with other students to commit to a class-based activity, then there is an increased chance they will not attend the session and slowly become increasingly disengaged with the course and its content. Therefore, spotting disharmony in your class is essential if you are going to create a sense of unity and functionality to proceedings and avoid the tensions that could arise as an alternative.

An impression of oneness can motivate feelings of shared progress and unity, and a heightened sense of identity also has a strong correlation with attitudes such as commitment – commitment to the group you share an identity with, but also commitment to the course and its content more generally. These positive attitudes are often closely related to each other, and commitment to the course may also inspire engagement with the content of the course. For a student to engage with a deep sense of learning, they will need to develop a similar level of commitment, and forging identities with the course and their own peers can help to promote this.

4.1.2   Developing Identities Online

While there are many benefits to online broadcasting, accompanying these are additional challenges to developing a sense of community and belonging among our students. The move to design and deliver specialist online courses has increased, with the demand for online programs and the development of Massive Online Open Courses (MOOCs) over recent times meaning that universities have taken up the opportunities to reach large audiences without some of the logistical challenges of in-person teaching. More recently, the disruption caused by the Covid pandemic meant an abrupt switch to online learning for many academics who were ill-prepared – an experience also witnessed by their students, who found the transition to online teaching equally challenging.

While managing the steep learning curve of how we could adapt our teaching to make use of the various online platforms constituted our main immediate challenge, it became obvious that the absence of the essential elements of community building through in-person social presence was a problem of a similar magnitude. In many instances, students found this led to difficulties forming and maintaining identities and, for some, to feelings of alienation, with the inevitable detrimental impact on student confidence levels and their engagement with learning more generally.

While we have now returned to some of the more traditional ways of delivering our teaching, many programs have held on to the positive aspects that emerged from the switch to online learning. For some courses this has led to a more blended approach that allows students to return to campus-based teaching and form those essential bonds enabled by a social presence, while also benefiting from some elements of online delivery that have supported and improved the overall learning experience. In these cases where digital communication of learning content and materials complements in-person teaching, there is less chance that student identity and engagement will be impacted.

However, the increase in purpose-built online-only programs poses more of a challenge for educators in trying to build a sense of community with and among their students, which puts at risk the development of important attitudes such as student engagement and commitment to the program. In a similar vein to some employees who prefer working remotely, where students choose to study purely online it is quite possible that these students will be trying to juggle other commitments. While trying to respond to program demands, other commitments could include looking after family, other caring duties, and full-time or part-time work. Where this is the case, developing social presence online is still possible but becomes more challenging to the uninitiated as difficulties arise in utilizing group synergies when the verbal and nonverbal cues that we rely on during in-person teaching are missing. As we already know, interactive participation is important toward developing engagement, but it also forms part of the student journey toward a deeper level of learning. For example, study groups will find the verbal and nonverbal cues I refer to much more conducive toward building synergies within the group.

Of course, this will depend on the student, and while some students will not feel such a need to build connections with the group and so more easily manage the lack of in-person social presence, others will find this missing social presence a barrier to their learning experience. Work-arounds to form an online social presence will be enough for some students, while others will feel emotionally and psychologically challenged by the potential isolation of learning purely online, in more extreme cases leading to disengagement and leaving the program. This is where learning management systems or virtual learning environments can become essential elements of our teaching toolkit and offer an efficient and effective way of communicating with and within student groups. I will talk more about the efficient and effective use of learning management systems in Part II of the book.

4.2   CONSIDERATION OF INCLUSIVE PRACTICE

While we are designing courses to maximize student engagement, inclusive practice should be a top priority. If not, we risk alienating some students from the outset, and once this happens it may be difficult to encourage them back on board. Yet, before we consider how to incorporate inclusive practice into the course framework, we need to recognize that diversity is multifaceted and establish which groups are most likely to need our support. For example, students of different ethnicities, cultures, educational background, and socio-economic status are likely to arrive at university with dissimilar expectations and levels of confidence. Socio-economic status[3] could have an impact on the quality of pre-university education. Those students who are the first in their family to attend university (typically first-generation students) will miss the advantages of having an older sibling or family member who has already experienced the transition from secondary education to university.

In a similar vein, international students who have little cultural experience of the country they will be studying in may suffer a seismic shock when they eventually encounter reality and arrive in their destination country. Certainly, contextual circumstances that the student will encounter, such as the quality of secondary education and social inequalities that exist within a given society, have been found to have a long-standing effect on achievement, something that can persist throughout a child's education and learning in later years. As program directors and course tutors it is important to be aware of inclusive practice and the need to devise more equitable ways of both teaching and offering opportunities to students. In doing so we can help students to improve their self-efficacy and to forge a better sense of identity, factors that will be important for them to reach the level of engagement that is necessary to succeed.

4.2.1   The Merits of Participation

While it is widely acknowledged that university can be a great leveler, this cannot necessarily be said of the students' educational experience before this point. For a variety of reasons I have already alluded to, students will arrive on their program with various levels of motivation and commitment. Students who struggle to feel a sense of community and fail to start forming their identities early on may be more reluctant to step up to the plate and participate in your teaching sessions, which means that not only will they be missing the learning benefits from making their own contribution, but other students present will also miss the benefits from that contribution. It is recognized that participation is a critical element of effective pedagogical and andragogical[4] learning and, indeed, makes an important contribution toward students taking ownership of their learning.

Students who participate in classroom discussion can receive feedback on their understanding and check their learning through the process of sensemaking (i.e., making sense of the current discussion by confirming their understanding via tutor feedback). They can also benefit from sharing ideas with their peers and building on the debate, inspiring others to make further contributions. Through the eyes of a student, participation can be seen as learning through trial and error (i.e., you may answer the question incorrectly), which may be of little concern to some students, but will frighten the life out of others. That is why you need to work hard to gain the trust of the group and show them they are operating in a safe environment where it is OK to get something wrong. Class participation also helps students engage with a deeper form of learning by entering the process of interpreting information, analyzing, and forming opinions or evaluating the content of the discussion, and therefore going beyond a dependence on more simplistic strategies for surface learning such as memory retention (White, 2011).

So, we can see that student participation can aid skills development in the form of critical thinking, problem solving, and reflective practice, but it will also help to form a more complete classroom discussion that will benefit the whole teaching group. We should not underestimate how important these forums are in the cultivation of important soft skills that will be directly transferable to the workplace. This includes their role in developing communication skills through debating and group interaction, along with the opportunity they provide for learning to manage other dynamics of group working. As Opie et al. (2019) highlight, classroom behavior often resembles the power and politics witnessed in wider society.

Where this type of classroom behavior prevails, minority groups that feel less inclined to contribute can develop the aura of an out-group as they watch on from the periphery of the class, feeling apprehensive about being judged or evaluated by their peers. Where this becomes the norm, there is a danger that they will find it increasingly difficult to engage with the group and their learning development may be checked in the ways I refer to above.

4.2.2 The Challenge for Minorities

How groups behave in wider society can have a significant part to play in learning about our classroom demographic in the form of participation and engagement levels. As experienced educators we need to know how to work the room and make sure we adopt an inclusive approach to class discussions.

What do I mean by this? Well, by making sure you focus attention on students who do not have the dominant voice you will be making sure those who are reluctant to participate are encouraged to do so, thereby improving the quality of your teaching sessions in all the ways I have previously identified. You will need to be conscious of subtly reducing the presence of those with a dominant voice and increasing the presence of others who are taking a more passive approach to participation in your class discussions.

One more point: while the visible characteristics of the group help us to identify its demography and are a factor that could result in some students feeling isolated or in a minority, there are aspects of diversity that are not so visible. An example of this is the presence of learning impediments, where students with such impediments may also feel isolated among the wider group because their additional challenges (e.g., pace of reading, writing, or processing of new knowledge in various formats) are not always understood or considered when we are setting classroom activities or prep work to be completed out of class.

It is important we understand that while some or many of these factors will be present, each group will have a nuance of its own that will influence the dynamic of the class. For example, group norms, including societal norms, will have some influence over how each cohort behaves. This will mean having to adjust behavior for some students, particularly in the first few weeks of teaching. As the tutor you have some responsibility to ensure your classes are inclusive for all, and through exercising this responsibility you can positively influence student engagement.

4.2.3   Inclusivity and Online Delivery

As alluded to earlier, online delivery of teaching can pose additional challenges regarding issues surrounding inclusive practice and building student identities, as well as motivation, which, inevitably, risks impacting student engagement. So, it is also valuable to consider the additional challenges involved in ensuring an inclusive teaching environment when resorting to online learning.

During the recent Covid pandemic, some countries resorted to part or full online delivery of their university programs. I am sure we are all aware of the opportunities but also issues this presented for some students (and tutors), not least the difficulties of helping the student to feel connected with the wider cohort and teaching team, and therefore the problems of helping them to build identities.

However, for some students synchronous online teaching provides the benefit of removing the large classroom environment and its daunting nature, particularly for a number of those in the minority groups I refer to above. During online delivery, most of the interactive and problem-solving elements of the seminar or workshop format are conducted in break-out groups, which tend to be more intimate and, with the tutor hopping from group to group, can be less daunting for minority groups when responding to questions or entering discussions with both peers and tutors within an unobtrusive and less evaluative environment. From this perspective, synchronous online teaching can be construed as more inclusive than in-person group teaching.

Even so, drawing from my own experience and anecdotal evidence from the many conversations I have had with teaching colleagues, it is much easier for students to 'hide' in online sessions and hence it becomes almost impossible to carry out the exercise of scanning the room and be empathetically aware of each student and conscious of their disposition. For those students who chose an on-campus experience and found themselves having to revert to online, this may well have challenged and exacerbated inclusivity and their previous efforts in forming an identity with their peers, resulting in feelings of alienation. This risked compounding the lower levels of motivation and engagement experienced by many. Alternatively, for students who choose to study online it is easy to underestimate the loneliness of being apart from your peers and not being able to experience the in-person identity-building process that I discussed earlier in this chapter.

In Part II of the book I will go on to discuss what we can do as course tutors to make our classes feel like more inclusive environments and some techniques for improving inclusiveness for online teaching delivery.

4.3   ENCOURAGING INTERACTION

In the last section I discussed the importance of student participation. Not only are participation and interaction similar constructs in the sense that both are prerequisites of student engagement, and vital ingredients of identity building with both peers and academics, but they are also consequential toward our effort to develop an inclusive teaching practice. More specifically, generating a better form of participation and interaction with both peers and tutors can aid sensemaking through the process of shared meaning, an essential part of student learning. However, in this context I am referring only to in-class participation.

To be clear about the specifics of what I am referring to in this instance by 'interaction' it will be helpful to visit Hillman et al.'s (1994) framework. Hilman et al. defined interaction by considering four different dyadic relationships: 1) learner–teacher, 2) learner–content, 3) learner–learner, and 4) learner–interface. The fourth component of the framework (learner–interface) relates to the relationship – one which is of increasing importance as an andragogical tool in higher education – between the learner and different technological mediums, including learning management systems, which may have relevance to either distance or blended forms of learning. Let us now consider some of the imperatives of healthy interaction and how they lend themselves to a quality student learning experience.

4.3.1   Promoting Positive Attitudes

Earlier research about both peer and tutor interaction highlights the benefits that cognitive, emotional, and social interactions can bring to the learner in the form of better learning outcomes and increased student satisfaction (e.g., see Wells, 1999). In this sense, cognitive interaction refers to the student's personal investment in learning characterized by their psychological state (e.g., how much effort and persistence they put into studying the subject). In addition to feelings of identity and belonging that they have developed during their time on the course, emotional interactions include how students feel in relation to learning tasks and, more generally, within the class environment (boredom, interest, happy, anxious, etc.).

An increase in student satisfaction (an example of a positive attitude) may become evident where we see instances of collaborative interaction in group work or interaction at a more intense level between student and tutor, supporting understanding through feedback and interpretation of any content being discussed. Students who are more satisfied with their program are more likely to go on and achieve positive outcomes in higher education. Advanced levels of interaction leading to increased social presence for students has also been recognized for its value in increasing student satisfaction (Richardson et al., 2017).

Where there is a lack of personal interaction there is also evidence that this can be detrimental to student outcomes. A lack of interaction with peers and tutors has been found to be a key source of student dissatisfaction while, inevitably, the lack of interaction leads to a reduction in the amount of feedback the student will receive from peers and tutors (Cole et al., 2014; Muuro et al., 2014).

More generally, a student's level of interest in the course and the level of experience they have gathered in the subject field, from either an academic or practical perspective, will also increase the prospects of interaction. It makes sense that previous experience of a topic can help the student feel as though they are on more confident ground when it comes to class discussion or raising questions, whether in-person or when using online forums or chat rooms connected to the course learning management system. Past experience may also include the level at which a student has previously engaged in a particular subject within a practical setting. For example, students who have experience from internships or part-time work can bring learnings from that experience into the classroom environment. These experiences can also provide useful examples as engaging stories for other students to learn from in the form of peer learning within the classroom.

Positive outcomes for students from their increased interaction and engagement can be experienced in a variety of ways, such as an enhanced level of academic learning, a greater degree of critical awareness, and being more prepared to take responsibility for their own learning. Increased interaction and engagement also increases levels of perseverance, improving the likelihood of a student becoming more resilient to adverse events and fulfilling the requirements of their program.

4.3.2   Proximal and Distal Interaction

Zimmerman et al. (2018) recognize the importance of what they refer to as 'immediacy behaviors'[5] and their ability to improve the quality of in-class communication while also increasing the likelihood of student engagement. Examples of the tutor using verbal forms of immediacy behaviors include using and extending student examples in class discussion, referring to students by their name, and using humor in class. Examples of the tutor using nonverbal immediacy behavior include smiling, using a relaxed body posture, and using spatial proximity to mingle with the student group as opposed to remaining within a given territory at the front of the class.

The visual presence of both students and tutors will help with community building and is particularly important at the outset of a course where identities have not yet been formed between the student and others on their course. Visibility allows simple things such as eye contact, body language, and other outward expressions that provide us with signals about the other person's emotional and cognitive state. If we flip this and consider a situation where physical presence is missing, it becomes much more challenging for the student to notice signals from the classroom, including signals being expressed by members of their peer group.

Earlier I mentioned the importance of cognitive, emotional, and social inter-action in relation to learning outcomes for students. Of course, one of the challenges associated with a purely online mode of learning that lacks in-person presence is for the tutor to find ways of both assessing and remedying the cognitive and emotional needs of the student. This is made even more demanding if students are reluctant to turn on their web cameras, meaning a physical presence goes undetected. This makes it difficult for the tutor to interact and forge a relationship with the student and for the student and their peers to build community and group identity. It may well be that the students who are most reluctant to make themselves visible are those experiencing the biggest issues with their cognitive and emotional needs. In online forums where all students opt to leave their cameras switched off, the only person they will be able to see on-screen is the tutor. In these situations, the benefits of working in small groups are lost (i.e., it really does not matter if 20 students or 200 students have joined the session). All the benefits that a student can gain from interacting with their group are lost, particularly where students only communicate via the online chat function as opposed to using their audio.

Situations such as these where students 'hide' within the group and choose isolation over interaction have been known to lead to decreased motivation and an increase in mental stress, boredom, and fatigue. In-class communication between student and tutor that is supported by active participation is one of the best ways of developing student engagement. If the preferred option is to teach online, then methods of adapting the online course to counteract some of these challenges are imperative for building and maintaining student engagement through the delivery of effective, quality communication. Otherwise, there is a risk of encountering problems with each antecedent of engagement that I have outlined so far in this chapter (i.e., inclusivity, identity, positive attitude development, developing social presence, and building community).

However, you will be pleased to know that it is possible to maintain standards of teaching quality and provide effective learning via online-only delivery if content, assessment, and teaching methods are adapted to accommodate effective communication, stimulate interaction, and build student engagement. In these circumstances, where the predominant form of delivery is online, student evaluation and feedback become even more critical for learning about what worked and what did not work so well.

Student interaction is core to student engagement, and I will talk more about the strategies for improving interaction, both where in-person teaching methods are used and where online teaching methods have been adopted, in Part II of the book.

4.4   BUILDING TRUST IN THE TUTOR–STUDENT RELATIONSHIP

Past studies have offered evidence of a direct positive correlation between the quality of the tutor–student relationship and the academic achievement of the student (e.g., Furrer and Skinner, 2003). The quality of this relationship can also have positive influences on student motivation and attitudes, such as student satisfaction, self-efficacy, and student engagement (Sakiz et al., 2012). A good tutor–student relationship will encourage students to be assertive in seeking more support with their learning by, for example, becoming more interactive in class or having more frequent contact with their tutor to check their understanding and learning (e.g., visiting the tutor during their academic support hours). In the main, they are more likely to employ a consistent approach to raising questions either online or in person.

A good relationship could also help to improve the student's self-efficacy, encouraging the student to take more responsibility for managing their own learning. These are all behaviors that help direct the student to higher achievement. We really can make a meaningful contribution to student goal achievement!

4.4.1   Leading through Trust

So, while it is recognized that the relationship students foster with their peers is fundamental to identity and engagement building, it is also correct to say something similar about the relationship they build with you as their tutor. But no meaningful relationship can be developed without the ingredient of mutual trust. The level of trust built through rapport with your students will also entice better engagement, better performance, and other positive student outcomes.

Because of the link with better engagement, building a trusting rapport with your students is particularly important for those who are new to university and just starting out on their program. It will reduce the chance that they will disengage and become at risk of dropping out from university. Attrition tends to be higher at the beginning of a program and so extra effort here will reap dividends by helping the student get off to a good start with your course while also keeping them on board with the wider program.

Trust can be seen as generalized (i.e., trusting in nature) or more specific (dependent on particular characteristics). Past studies have shown that the trustworthiness of a tutor can lead to an increase in out-of-class contact, perhaps to ask questions over email or to visit the tutor during their student support hours (for examples, see Dobransky and Frymier, 2004; Jaasma and Koper, 1999).

4.4.2   Trusting Your Judgment

You have a big responsibility. While most students will naturally trust your judgment about how you have designed your course, it helps to explain the delivery structure at the outset: why this makes sense in relation to the course aims. For example, why you have built in more (or fewer) lectures than other courses on the program; why your course follows a workshop format and how this differs from a seminar format; what additional content or support material is delivered through the learning management system and other technological support systems, and why it may be necessary for students to engage with this content and complete any pre-learning in advance of the taught sessions; how the students will be assessed, how frequently, and how this aligns with the teaching activities and the course learning outcomes (I will say more about this in Part II).

Students like to know why they are being asked to follow a particular course of action and if you take time out to explain these details to them it helps with their sensemaking. Knowing that you have designed the course in a format to support their learning in the best conceivable way will also help to support that early trust-building process.

It is often the case in undergraduate teaching that I have been asked 'but what has this got to do with me getting a good mark in my assessment?' You need to challenge a student's perspective that class activity should be developed with the single objective of preparing them for the summative assessment and, instead, emphasize their need to connect with the wider course objectives. While it is true that content needs to align with the andragogical aims and objectives, and the link between learning and assessment is a critical element of a well-designed course, it should not become the sole factor of consideration during course design.

4.4.3   Our Dedication to the Cause

Students will also want to trust that their tutors have their best interest at heart when designing and organizing the course content and delivery.[6] Faranda (2015) ascertained a relationship between tutors who demonstrate what is perceived to be a genuine sense of care for the students' interests and well-being (i.e., those tutors who will readily respond to students' learning needs), and an improvement in student engagement with out-of-class communication (e.g., raising questions outside the class via email or by visiting the tutor during their student support hours). This is another illustration of increasing student engagement through actions determined by you, the tutor, when leading by example.

Accordingly, a student's trust in you before they set off on that journey of learning will be contingent on how well you can demonstrate:

1.   your own mastery of and passion for the subject;
2.   that you are committed to helping support them to achieve their objectives of learning.

Bringing the students on board through them knowing they can rely on your support and that you will present an accurate depiction of the subject content is an essential characteristic of building that trusting relationship between student and tutor. The effectiveness of the course design, which is a reflection of the quality of its organization and delivery as determined by the structure of the teaching, the course content, and the way the course is assessed, will also help to build a student's trust in you, the course leader.

4.5   CHAPTER SUMMARY

In Chapter 4 I have set out some of the key challenges surrounding student engagement and how we, as educators, can try to overcome these. The main steps to promote better student engagement include helping the student to forge an identity with the course, making sure they feel included, and encouraging participation and interaction with their peers, their tutors, and the platforms we use in our teaching. I have brought this all together in Figure 4.1 and identified each of these items as a central pillar of student engagement. You will see how I recognize the inter-related nature of each pillar and their combined impact on student engagement.

Of course, some programs are far less likely to encounter problems with students who are reluctant to interact. While that is not always the case, even when it is, at the outset undergraduate freshers tend to be more reticent about getting involved with in-class discussion, and this forms close links with some of the content I covered in Chapter 3 about confidence and student mindset. However, issues still exist at postgraduate level, where diversity and inclusivity may be more of a challenge to manage. There will be some postgraduate programs (I am thinking particularly in terms of MBA students) where interaction will not be such an issue, due to the students' past experiences (e.g., from their working environment or previous encounters in higher education).

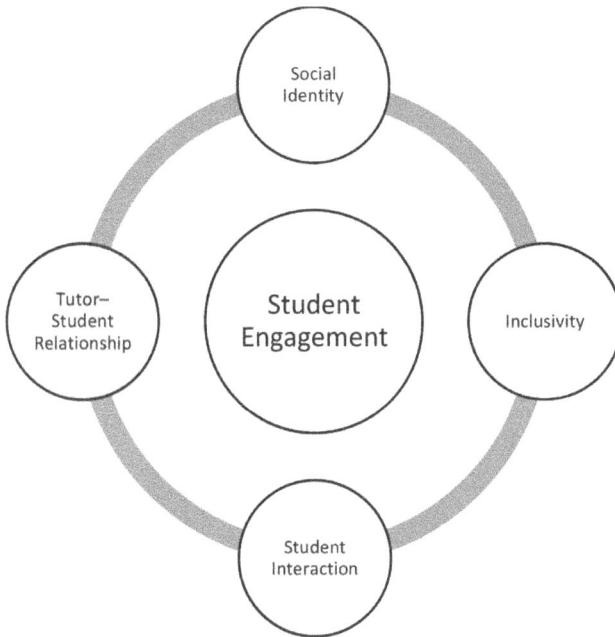

Figure 4.1   The central pillars of student engagement

In this chapter I have also included content on digital forms of learning, where engagement has proved to be more of a challenge. While educators developing purpose-built online programs may be fully conscious of the additional challenges around student engagement and how their courses can be designed to take account of this, there is a danger that it is not a central consideration for blended courses, where a mix of in-person and digital delivery is incorporated.

In Chapter 5 I bring Part I of the book to a close by focusing on the all-important topic of skills development, and, once again, consider what you need to know about your students before you sign off on the design of your new or revised course.

NOTES

1.   Enabling the student to understand a clear link between their own goals, the course learning objectives, and the program learning objectives. Explaining how each form of assessment aligns with the course learning outcomes also helps to equip the student with clarity and understanding. The significance of aligning these components is discussed at greater length in Part II of the book.
2.   That is, who we are and who we might want to become.

3. Often measured using parents' occupation and education, which will identify whether the student is first-generation higher education.
4. The terms 'pedagogy' and 'andragogy' are used to label approaches to learning at different life stages. Pedagogy is associated with learning in childhood, where the student plays more of a passive role and is dependent on the teacher. Andragogy is associated with adult forms of learning. The student is expected to become a more independent learner, demonstrating autonomy and self-direction.
5. In this instance, the term 'immediacy behaviors' refer to the use of verbal and nonverbal cues that increase closeness in communication.
6. For example, drawing from the most up-to-date concepts in the specialist field and ensuring the content includes relevant and recent examples.

5. Skills development

5.1 INTRODUCTION

The expectations of a university education have experienced a shift in emphasis over the past two decades. Long gone are the days when a degree was solely recognized as a way for students to improve their minds. With skills shortages on the agenda and employers worldwide highlighting the skills gap for those entering the job market, the role of universities has become more important than ever. Employers identify the skills gap as a global phenomenon, with studies identifying a gap between some aspects of graduate education and skills that are usable in the workplace both across the West (e.g., see Humburg et al., 2017) and in other large economies, such as China (Ren et al., 2011) and South Africa (Horwitz, 2013).

As disseminators of knowledge, one of our primary functions in higher education is to promote and support the imparting of skills among our students. Guidance about the skills agenda should be instigated at program level and emphasized to course leaders, who then need to be actively encouraged to integrate the learning of these skills into their course design. Raising awareness of which skills need to be included can be as straightforward as embedding them within the program learning outcomes and/or developing a list of transferable skills that are relevant to the program,[1] but it is important that, in some form, they are clearly communicated to course leaders. This is an example of where good program functionality via effective intra-program communication is essential, so that all course leaders are aware not only of the program learning outcomes and transferable skills but also of where they are being covered (or not being covered) elsewhere in the program. This ensures that course leaders concentrate on developing the range of skills across the spectrum while also avoiding over-duplication of effort where some learning outcomes and transferable skills are covered in abundance and deficiencies where there is only sparse coverage of others. It is also important to bear in mind that if we are to build programs aimed at maximizing student potential, we also need to equip them with skills that can help overcome the challenges of social inequalities and support them to develop strong networks that will provide them with the interpersonal contacts needed to get on after graduation.

Today, upskilling in preparation for the recruitment market is one of the most compelling arguments for choosing to study at university. The skills employers need students to be equipped with once they are installed in the working environment may well depend on the type of industry and the specific job roles in question. However, there are other skills deemed to be critical to the employability process that precede the recruitment stage. These skills are more akin to how well students promote and situate themselves in society, particularly among networks that will be supportive of them in their search for graduate recruitment. They are often referred to as positioning and process skills.

In Chapter 2 I introduced a framework of different types of capital as presented through the lens of human capital theory. These different types of capital are formed by the accumulation of various skills, and I explained how this capital, and therefore these skills, can make the student more appealing to prospective employers. Correctly, you may consider it to be the central role of a careers advisor or personal tutor to support students as they work toward developing these skills at university. However, there are some simple adjustments we can build into our courses to support students who have not yet had the chance to cultivate these incredibly important skills. If we do not, there is a risk that while we resource students with the practical skills employers are seeking, they may still be ill-prepared for the challenges they will encounter during recruitment and selection in a highly competitive graduate jobs market.

In this chapter I want to spend some time outlining the skills we need to consider when building our courses and programs. My priorities here will not be specific technical skills, because they will be unique to your own program and course requirements, but more the generic skills that are transferable and can be applied in most graduate job markets. These skills are what many students choosing to go to university will be seeking to develop.

While you will not be able to incorporate all the skills I will mention, it makes sense to focus on those that are most suited to your modes of delivery and the teaching content of your course. I am also communicating this message to program directors whose job it will then be to scan the range of skills embedded within the courses on your program and make sure you are working with your program team to ensure synergies by building a program that incorporates the range of employability skills needed for the graduate jobs market pertaining to your wider discipline.

I will draw upon Holmes's (2013) three-component model of employability skills for my main inspiration in this chapter. As you can see in Figure 5.1, the model is presented as a skills development framework, incorporating possession skills, positioning skills, and process skills. The framework helps us to develop a more comprehensive approach to understanding skills development and the broad range of skills that students will seek to develop during their university journey – skills that can be identified as educational outcomes.

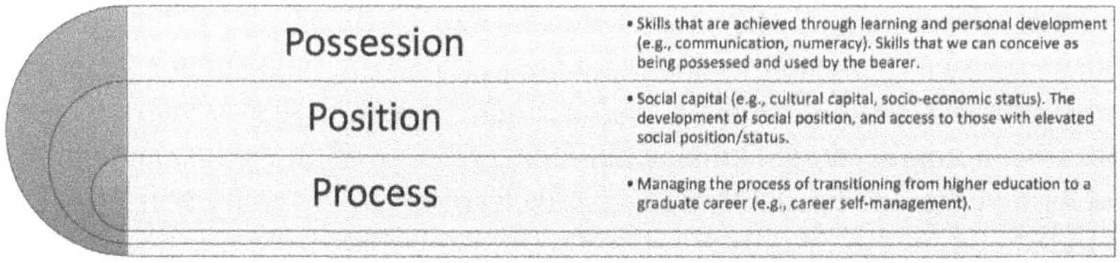

Possession	• Skills that are achieved through learning and personal development (e.g., communication, numeracy). Skills that we can conceive as being possessed and used by the bearer.
Position	• Social capital (e.g., cultural capital, socio-economic status). The development of social position, and access to those with elevated social position/status.
Process	• Managing the process of transitioning from higher education to a graduate career (e.g., career self-management).

Source: Holmes (2013).

Figure 5.1   Employability skills – the three-component model

While I will explain each of the three components of Holmes's model in the next section, briefly: *possession skills* are those that we own, accumulate, and regularly use; *positioning skills* help us to understand how we relate to society in terms of social standing and social awareness; and *process skills* help the individual engage more effectively with the employment process and refer to the self-management of career advancement. Together, these are the skills that will help prepare our students for graduate recruitment. You will also be familiar with many of these skills, but not necessarily so in relation to the content and delivery of our own course. Hopefully, I can encourage you to think through how you can play your part in promoting these skills. I will discuss each of these in turn, beginning with possession skills. It is possible that you already have a plan regarding how to integrate them into your course.

5.2   POSSESSION SKILLS

Broadly, these are the skills that we develop and hone over time, usually through repetition, training, and modeling ourselves on others (social learning), but also through individual study and collaborative working. While students look to advance these skills during their time at university and become well-equipped with them at the point of graduation, they will also have developed some of the skills to a rudimentary level before starting the university journey. For example, the student's level of interpersonal, communication, and analytical skills could be dependent on their formative years, and they may also be dependent on inherited traits and so could be personality dependent too.

Possession skills become part of our armory and help define who we are and our strengths and weaknesses (e.g., excellent communicator, analytical mind, good at problem solving). They tend to be transferable between situations and are therefore valued by employers. Moreover, this category includes technical skills developed for a particular career or job role, and so there is often the added benefit that industry competitors also value them.

Possession skills will include the learning undertaken on a particular program or course and the theoretical and practical aspects of the subject content learned, but also the skills that are necessary to help support learning (e.g., critical thinking, reading, and writing; digital analysis; interpersonal skills, including debating skills; negotiation; group-working skills; and verbal and written presentation). Of course, skills learning at university will likewise include learning those skills required for applying many of the expected academic conventions, such as referencing and source recognition through in-text citations, the art of essay writing, reflective writing, report writing, and so on, which may also be significant to post-graduation destinations. The expected level of proficiency in each of these skills could be dependent on a variety of factors, but employers will look to universities to turn out students equipped with a rounded skill set sufficient to meet the demands of the graduate jobs market.

While most employers will hope to see a return on higher-end skills when investing in graduate recruits, they will also be hoping that some of the more basic skills have not been overlooked. For example, while a student may know how to produce a great essay and achieve high marks in assessment, can they produce an email that hasn't been carelessly constructed to be misconstrued as lacking respect or, in the worst case, offensive? This can be of equal importance to an employer who needs to know the student will have the gravitas not to give a bad impression to their clients when representing the organization. Whereas most employers are not so fussed about the new or potential recruit's referencing skills or if they can construct a good essay, they will value a critical thinker – someone who can think creatively, challenging convention and seeking new and more efficient ways of doing things. The value of the skills will be dependent on the role the employer is asking the graduate to fulfill, but the point is that the basics really do matter at all levels of study.

5.2.1   The Employer Perspective

Have you ever wondered why some employers seem to have a constant presence on some university campuses, an indomitable presence at recruitment fairs, a team of on-campus student brand ambassadors, regular seminar and workshop presentations, the most generous offerings of internships, and an excellent relationship with career advisors and faculty employability teams? Well, it is usually because the university has been a good recruiting ground for them in the past, producing a steady stream of reliable and well-prepared students for the graduate roles they have in mind. Ambitious and hungry students who are equipped with the right skill sets and therefore ready to hit the ground running when they graduate usually provide a steady stream of young talent for the organization. The market-value capital of potential new recruits is that which is most prized by employers.[2]

Therefore, the alignment between the skills that graduates possess and those necessary for the roles being recruited by an organization is in the interest of both the job candidate and the organization or its recruiting department. So, your time spent as course leader working on developing skills such as critical thinking, communication (written and oral), decision-making, creativity, initiative, resilience, and many more besides will be helping students to build a skill profile much sought after by organizations globally. Your contribution is important because it helps to support the scaffolding process of skills building during the student's time on their program. A coherent program built around a cohesive program team should be able to emphasize the synergies offered by this layered approach to skills building.

5.2.2   Embedding into Deep Learning

Many of the skills, such as those required to tackle different forms of academic writing (e.g., essay, reflective writing), and academic conventions, such as critical thinking and referencing, can be taught in dedicated professional development skills (PDS) courses offered during the early part of a program. Yet, other course leaders can also have an essential role by offering students the chance to put these skills into practice during formative and summative assessment exercises. It is essential that some form of dedicated training via a PDS course is offered to students in the early weeks of their program if they are to be equipped with the skills that will be necessary to produce their first formative or summative written assessments to a given standard. Additionally, other courses that form part of the student's program – that is, non-PDS ones – could also include professional and personal development skill-building activity, which will help to tap into some of the positioning and process skills that I will come on to talk about shortly.

To be truly effective and give the students a chance to both practice and deep learn those skills, whenever a PDS course is embedded into the initial stages of a program, its learning outcomes must also be integrated into the learning objectives of other courses operating at the same level of the program. As the PDS course helps students to develop the range of academic skills needed to support their learning on the program, this interconnectivity with other course assignments will allow these skills to become entrenched via the feedback received after applying them in practice during formative and summative assessment. This helps the student engage with the process of deep learning through active engagement.

At this point, it might be helpful to understand the concept of deep learning as a holistic cyclical process developed around a sequence of events, such as the experiential learning process offered by David Kolb (2014).[3] Kolb recognized that learning was incomplete unless it included each of four inter-connected stages, including what he referred to as 'active experimentation.' Being able to contextualize the skills learning through active experimentation is essential to enable consolidation of this new knowledge. It is also important for the tutor to make the student aware that they are engaging with that skill at the point of learning (offering different arguments to form a critical approach; giving reasons for differences of opinion during teamworking tasks; etc.).

Perhaps this is more for the attention of program directors, but if it is not possible logistically to dedicate a credit-bearing module to professional development skills then, at the very least, you should consider allowing students access to non-credit-bearing PDS training, even if this is offered more generically as a form of inter-program skills development package (i.e., in collaboration with other program directors). While the training may not be tailored toward your program, it may be a more practical way of including an activity of this kind. By offering PDS training to all students on your program, it will help them to build a more consistent approach when cultivating learning strategies and applying academic conventions.

5.3   POSITIONING SKILLS

While universities inevitably focus on helping their students to develop, hone, and fine-tune the possession skills I refer to above, societal positioning (how one relates to the social systems one operates within) can become a critical factor during job search. Social positioning can help job seekers to identify opportunities and to make connections with the gatekeepers of those opportunities. Cultural and social capital, which is often borne from socio-structural inequalities (e.g., unfair legal, educational, and economic systems) and socio-political (power distribution) inequalities, tend to be monopolized by the dominant classes (those who have particular influence over knowledge, ideas, symbols, etc.). Let us take a closer look at these conceptions and their relationship with the search for graduate employability.

5.3.1   Developing Cultural and Social Capital

A key source for acquiring cultural capital can be family links or other connections within the close community one operates within (including education systems). An individual's elevated position within a given social field helps to generate a certain habitus that is typical of their position (i.e., a background system of shared understandings, perceptions, orientations, tastes, etc.), helping to characterize their social group and to prompt an internalization of the social group's patterns of behavior (e.g., speech, posture, attitudes, opinions). Where elitism exists within higher education systems, some would say that it is structured to reinforce social positioning and status. Advantages here may include mode of language, set of values, practices and rituals, and other perceived privileges that often become dependent upon class structure. In these systems the dominant class tends to preside over the rules, which, within a class-structured system, are already set to favor students from privileged backgrounds, ensuring that advantages for them are enabled within the system. Where this presides, the benefits of having access to a more privileged social background (e.g., access to more prestigious educational credentials) becomes institutionalized.

Within the structures of these social systems, social elites can position themselves where the supply of a commodity, such as social reach, acumen, and other possession skills, increases at a greater pace than demand. Therefore, such commodities are easily attained and applied to advantageous effect by those who have access to them. Some higher education systems are structured to reinforce social positioning and status. This is illustrated within the Possession–Position–Process (i.e., 3-Ps) framework.

The emancipatory communitarian framework (Prilleltensky, 1997) attempts to account for the societal and organizational factors that hinder people in a position of disadvantage (taking a social justice perspective) and negate some, or all, of the structural barriers that impinge on people's lives – in other words, the mechanisms that perpetuate oppression, maintain privilege, and preserve social inequalities. Assuming this perspective and applying the framework to the current context would encourage educators to take appropriate mitigating action to disturb these structural barriers that maintain the status quo.

Being aware of the potential impact from societal structures (some would say impediments) is important, although many would argue that universities have already developed systems to help overcome some of these inherent disadvantages for students who are not from the societal elite. It is argued that university is a great leveler, and there are certainly some good examples to support this argument, even though higher education has been recognized in some quarters as institutionally elite. However, while inter-institutional and intra-institutional elitism do undoubtedly exist, it is possible to mitigate the latter by making available opportunities for all, just so long as there is equal access to these opportunities for those students who wish to take them up.

In Chapter 2 I introduced a discussion about human capital theory, and the significance of positioning skills in the form of social and cultural capital, both highly valued by employers. A survey conducted in the UK by the CBI and Pearson Education (2016) highlighted that some 30 percent of employers were dissatisfied with graduates' intercultural awareness, and while this number is not necessarily alarming, it shows there is still much to be done by universities to increase cultural capital.[4]

While there is plenty we can do at course level to increase our students' awareness of social and cultural capital, this needs to be managed at program level as program directors can ensure a range of co-curricular opportunities are available and easy to access for all students. In Part II, I will move on to discuss the ways we need to ensure that course and program design work synergistically and support students to develop employability skills, including social and cultural capital.

5.4   PROCESS SKILLS

In this context, 'process' relates to the steps individuals take toward ownership of their own career destiny, that is, career self-management (CSM). Through our work in higher education, we can support our students to develop proactive career behaviors at an early stage, helping them to successfully engage with the opportunities that are offered on the program or via the student support systems offered by the faculty or university (e.g., employability hub, career center).

The process in question begins with the first tentative steps of identifying potential career interests before moving on to recruitment activity, such as developing a strong CV and understanding how to complete job applications to a high standard. But much more than this, CSM involves researching and gathering on a regular basis career-related information and planning how this can be utilized – so, being proactive in researching and gathering relevant information about labor markets, careers, and the world of work and then effectively acting on this information.

From the student's perspective it means understanding themselves and what type of career might interest them, recognizing their skills and personal attributes, and being able to utilize the information to identify roles they would be most suited to. It also involves being proactive in seeking support from relevant others who will be able to help the student make the right decisions, such as career advisors, potential employers and those working for them, family, friends, and the student's extended network (another example of where one's social capital can be utilized).

This leads to developing a closely aligned career identity, better person–organization/occupation fit, and the ability to adapt to, and cope with, future career transitions. There are benefits to knowing how to network and thereby increase access to relevant job vacancy information, which can be enhanced by those who are able to take advantage of social capital gained through their previously developed networks and contacts outside of the university. Here we can see the links with positioning skills that were discussed in the last section. In addition to helping extend reach to those external contacts and developing the maze of networks that are so critical to students, work experience acquired from lucrative internships while at university increases human capital, helps to foster a career identity, and improves the ability to be adaptable in the working environment.

Managing the process also depends on the quality of interaction developed by the candidate with their gatekeeper(s) (i.e., those individuals who can manage access to important others in the organization). Forming a graduate identity is part of the social process students go through when leaving university and moving on to the next stage: settling into their positions in employment. The process of moving on from higher education (or indeed any previous form of education) to becoming employed is one of shifting and forming new identities as one goes through the change in self-concept (how one classifies and relates to oneself).

We should not underestimate the role universities can play in this process through the provision of quality support functions, including a careers service, university alumni services, and employability and opportunity hubs. Students having access to good support facilities that can guide and advise them about early careers and encourage them to take up short- or longer-term internships is an essential feature of a quality higher education provider. Other core functions of these services should include raising awareness about opportunities (e.g., recruitment adverts; awareness of any on- or off-campus employer-led events), but also being proactive in guiding students toward self-management when beginning a job search, while completing applications, and during the selection process itself.

Typically, the expertise of these core professional services staff will be disseminated across programs as the staff become part of the teaching and learning environment either through delivering specialist courses or through contributing to the PDS course syllabus. Their integration into the teaching and learning experience can play an essential role in the process of helping students develop the transferable skills they will need for the early-, mid-, and post-recruitment and selection process.

5.4.1 Your Part in the Process

Each component of the triadic skills framework outlined in this chapter plays an essential role in the successful management of graduate recruitment, but while process skills tend to be generic to most careers, possession and positioning skills are often more specific to a type of career. While most universities offer students vital support and guidance programs, the quality of these programs will differ from institution to institution. It is common for programs to be externally evaluated based on the percentage of students that enter graduate employment or further study; again, this can vary quite radically. Whether a program has a successful record of getting their students into graduate-level work will be dependent on a range of factors, including the quality of support that students are offered to help them self-manage their careers during their time at university and beyond. It will also depend on students' willingness to assume responsibility for their career management.

We can aim to develop and inspire through specially designed skills development courses (e.g., PDS courses) that could transition into more advanced levels as students progress through various stages of the program. But the job of equipping students with employability skills must go beyond the syllabus of a single standalone course. There needs to be a coherent connection with the rest of the program delivery if these skills are to be embedded in a deeper form of learning. There are various ways you can play a part in your role as course leader, from simply raising awareness about the range of roles and careers in graduate employment that are open to those entering your subject field, to inviting industry professionals to help deliver a lecture or seminar/workshop and, in doing so, pass on their experiences of connecting with that sector or field.[5]

There are many ways of designing your course creatively to bring career identity into the teaching. While I will be moving on to a more detailed discussion about design in the next part of the book, you may find it helpful to spend some time thinking about how you could adapt selected content of your course to include discussions about the practical aspects of employment in your subject field, including potential careers and job roles that might be interesting to the students. An additional benefit of this is that if students are enthused by related careers and job roles, it may inspire a deeper engagement with your subject.

Supporting students to overcome the hurdles they sometimes encounter when trying to make successful connections with the gatekeepers of employment, whether this is during initial research, job applications, or the selection process itself, may be fundamental to their recruitment outcome. As educators, we should consider how we can make some contribution to supporting students in this process.

5.5   THE HOLISTIC APPROACH TO SKILLS BUILDING

Holmes's three-component framework helps us to understand the diverse types of skills needed by university students if they are to be best placed to find graduate-level work at the end of their program. Helping our students to achieve this is also important for us as educators, because employability rates may well be evaluated at faculty, school, or program level, attracting both internal and external scrutiny.

To this point I have commented on schemes that allow some form of work-integrated learning in the program of study, including short-term internships or longer-term schemes such as a year in industry. Summer schools and year-long study abroad schemes offer students invaluable opportunities for skill building, particularly for procuring the development of student cultural and social capital. For most programs, these schemes are identified as co-curricular, or extra-curricular; they do not form part of the compulsory curriculum for that program. However, some programs (e.g., language degrees) do include an internship or study abroad year as a compulsory element of the curriculum.

Additional co-curricular or extra-curricular opportunities, such as internships, study overseas, sports club membership, and other activities offered by the university, have a vital role to play in the student skill-building process and can complement other efforts we make within the curriculum. I always try to promote these additional activities and aim to encourage my personal tutees to start at least one extra activity outside of their studies. Many of these activities provide an opportunity for students to put into practice some of the skills discussed in their teaching groups, such as teamwork, leadership, and communication, in addition to providing some time out from their formal studies. They also provide a vehicle for students to interact outside of their study bubble and share a wide range of valuable experiences with other students.

So, when we think about skills development at university, it is helpful if we understand the process from a holistic perspective and extend our vision of student learning beyond the formal curriculum that we deliver to them. There is also a part of their life that we do not enter but can, nevertheless, bring into the classroom discussion when exemplifying concepts and theory. This element of the learning process is depicted in Figure 5.2, where you will see the means of processing the skills recognized in the 3-Ps framework. The end goal is to develop a more rounded student with a set of transferable skills who will be better equipped to compete within the arena of employability. In this diagram, employability is deemed to be the output because it will usually follow at the end of the graduate program and, as I discussed beforehand, is often cited as the primary objective of the student in deciding to invest their resources in university study.

5.6   WHICH SKILLS?

The challenges posed for education and training providers to help close the so-called employability–skills gap and meet the practical requirements of an employer will depend, in part, on the industry your course is related to. If you

Skills   **Means**   **Output**

Possession		Curricular		
Position		Co-curricular		Employability
Process		Extra-curricular		

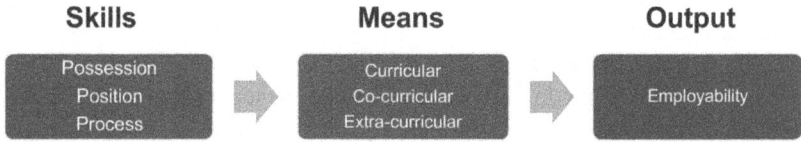

Figure 5.2   The higher education offer – capital development and return on capital

are a program director, you should have already developed an inventory of the key skills that will be most relevant to the students enrolled on your program. These will be identified in either the series of learning outcomes or the transferable skills presented in the program catalog listing. The learning objectives, outcomes, and competencies of your program should be recognized as the central determinators that help to shape the design of your program. If you are a course leader, once you have been given guidance from your program director on the overall objectives and expected outcomes of the program, you should be clear how best your course can contribute and decide which skills you need to focus on helping your students to develop.

While organizations will usually provide training for many of the job-specific technical skills, they will expect to see that more generic skills have already been embedded in the student's university program. The skills that many employers identify as lacking in graduate students tend to be the more generic soft skills that are often transferable between roles (e.g., general business acumen and effective interpersonal communication). This is where short- or longer-term internships can prove to be invaluable curricular or co-curricular options in a program, offering the student a chance to synergize their academic learning with practical experience.

At this stage, it may be helpful to consider the most sought-after core graduate attributes as identified in recent studies on this subject. Osmani et al. (2019) conducted their own systematic review of the literature to identify the skills, or attributes, that employers most want to see in their graduate recruits. Their study focused on just two sectors, the accounting & finance and ICT industries, and so the results are perhaps somewhat limited in their application. Even so, it provides some insight and understanding of the more generic soft skills that are most sought out by employers during the graduate recruitment process. As you may expect, the list is quite long and so I have included these in a table (Table 5.1) for ease of viewing.

According to the study, the top four interpersonal skills are communication, teamwork, problem solving, and creativity. The most sought-after applied skill is the ability to use technology. What is clear is that employers expect graduates to have developed these skills before beginning their term of employment

Table 5.1   *Core graduate attributes*

Graduate skills/attributes	Frequency of skill/ attribute being cited in the systematic literature review	Sources
Communication	24	Gray (2010)
Teamwork	18	Koppi et al. (2009)
Problem solving	11	Cox et al. (2013)
Technological	11	Nicolescu and Paun (2009)
Creativity	10	Jackson (2014)
Interpersonal	8	Azevedo et al. (2012)
Leadership	7	Ren et al. (2011)
Self-management	6	Moy (2006)
Flexibility/adaptability	6	Horwitz (2013)
Critical thinking	5	Scholarios et al. (2008)
Time management	5	
Willingness to learn	5	
Planning and organizing	5	
Initiative	4	
Negotiation	3	
Pre-graduation work experience	2	
Working under pressure	2	
Self-confidence	2	
Personality	2	
Independent working	2	
Motivation	2	

Source: Osmani et al. (2019).

and that it is, in part, the university's role to train graduates to be skills-ready when they start working for them rather than having to begin developing these skills when they arrive.

As Fraser et al. (2019) identify, 'at many institutions, employability skills appear in the employability profile, whereas the subject matter appears in the course learning outcomes where they form the focus of the course work and assessment' (p. 159). While I am sure this is often the case, there should be more of a conscious effort to incorporate practical engagement with the key employability skills within the course design, where they can appear in parallel alongside the teaching of other content. As I have already alluded to, developing a capstone course dedicated to skills teaching is important for any program but will be of little value unless the teaching of those skills is also embedded within the wider program, complemented with an ambition to offer students practical opportunities to experience using those skills. This scaffolding of learning through structured platforms that are purposefully integrated into the wider academic program will help to embed those capabilities, something that is particularly important in the initial stages of study. Learning many of these generic and transferable skills is often a tacit process. Relying on a process of learning purely delivered through standalone modules will not be enough, and a more holistic and pragmatic approach is needed.

5.7   CHAPTER SUMMARY

The central focus of Chapter 5 has been the all-important subject of skills development at university, with the chapter highlighting how both program directors and course leaders should work together to ensure students have opportunities to develop and practice a range of skills that will be important to them in their graduate careers. In introducing the theme of skills development I have drawn inspiration from Holmes's three-component framework. This encourages educators in higher education to look beyond possession skills and help prepare their students for graduate recruitment by assisting them in improving their societal positioning and equipping them with the skills they need when engaging with the recruitment process. I emphasized the influence we are capable of imparting in our role as educators and, subsequently, how we need to reflect on what we can deliver by designing our programs and courses to help support this range of skills development from a more holistic perspective. A key message is that unless we take a joined-up approach to program development and integrate more of the skills learning that students encounter in their PDS modules within the syllabus of other courses on the program, then the chance to embed these skills in a form of deep learning may well be missed.

5.8   SUMMARY OF PART I

My aim throughout Part I of this book has been to map out the journey of a student entering a program of higher education from the time of commitment to the early days of teaching and learning. In doing so I have emphasized some of the challenges the student will face and that may influence the range of behaviors that become manifested upon arrival at university. Some of the key issues that emerge around student confidence and engaging with the program of study are highlighted. I have also set out the students' expectations and, realistically, what we can do as educators in our attempt to meet those expectations. In connection with this point, I have dedicated Chapter 5 to discussing the key role we have to play in student skill development in preparedness for their graduate careers.

Drawing insight from human capital theory and Holmes's (2013) three-component framework, I have presented a range of ideas about what you could feasibly work into your own course to help embed some of the transferable skills I discussed in Chapter 5. I hope in doing so that I have given you some insight about what would work well for your students and how you may be able to contribute to their wider skills development. If so, this is an excellent outcome, and I am delighted that you are motivated to set out on this journey. However, despite any inspirational ideas you may have, you are only at the beginning of the journey and may now need some support in planning the next steps and delivering on your promises. In Part II of the book I will return to the key outcomes from Part I and show you how you can develop a series of tool-kits to implement the changes you will need to tweak behaviors and help instill the skills I have discussed. In short, I will outline the key stages of designing a course that focuses on supporting the student-oriented outcomes outlined in Part I, while understanding the needs of the contemporary university student.

NOTES

1. Course or program transferable skills can be designed for skills that are difficult to assess but are deemed to be an essential part of the overall course or program learning. They can be developed simultaneously with learning outcomes and can be used to complement learning outcomes, but whereas learning outcomes need to be formally assessed, transferable skills do not. Transferable skills should be identified in the course and program catalog entry as a separate sub-section to learning outcomes and will be helpful for students when they are reviewing course or program details. Learning outcomes and transferable skills are considered in more depth in Chapter 6.
2. See Chapter 2, Section 2.4 for a more detailed discussion.
3. I refer to Kolb's model of experiential learning in more detail in Chapter 8 when discussing assessment and feedback.
4. I also discuss cultural capital in Chapter 2, Section 2.4.
5. Having access to an initiative-taking and effective university alumni services team can be beneficial here.

PART II

Building the course

6. Course design: developing a framework

6.1   INTRODUCTION

A central aim of mine in Part I was to piece together some of the challenges experienced by a typical student entering higher education, helping to illustrate a culture that will incorporate an array of different personalities and social types, with the intention being to pave the way for the development of Part II. I do not pretend to provide a complete picture. The complexity of human nature makes this an impossible task. However, with supporting evidence from others working and publishing in the field of higher education, my aim has been to bring you into the student world, for this is the perspective we must take if we are to build courses and programs for higher education students that are both relevant and effective.

To either build or redesign a course there needs to be direction and a sense of purpose. I hope reading Part I of the book has given you a range of ideas about the pivotal role you can play in helping students overcome some of the barriers to learning they experience when planning your own course – from understanding the students' motivations (i.e., the reasons why they choose to come to university) and supporting them to grow in self-belief through maximizing their engagement, to helping them build a new social identity and teaching them new skills that will be critical to their future independence and successes in life. I want us now to return to those essential elements from Part I as I present a structure that you can apply to build your course from the ground upwards. In this context, the ground represents where the students are when they enter your course. The journey upward represents the newfound confidence you will provide them with, the skills you will help them to develop, and the vision you will instill regarding how they can also implement these new tools either to make further progress at the next level of learning or when they transition to life after graduation.

It is helpful to imagine this as a process of learning for the student – a change in circumstance for the learner, who will need to transition from their current state to a desired state where their learning and development has progressed satisfactorily. To reach their desired state, there will be several challenges to overcome. This change in circumstance can be effectively represented by borrowing from Kurt Lewin's (1943) force-field analysis of change and emphasizing some of the key factors that will help the learner to make the transition while also acknowledging the barriers that could impede their progress and either slow down their journey or block the pathway altogether. In this latter case, no progress is possible until the barriers have been removed or significantly reduced in magnitude. A visual representation of this concept is presented in Figure 6.1.

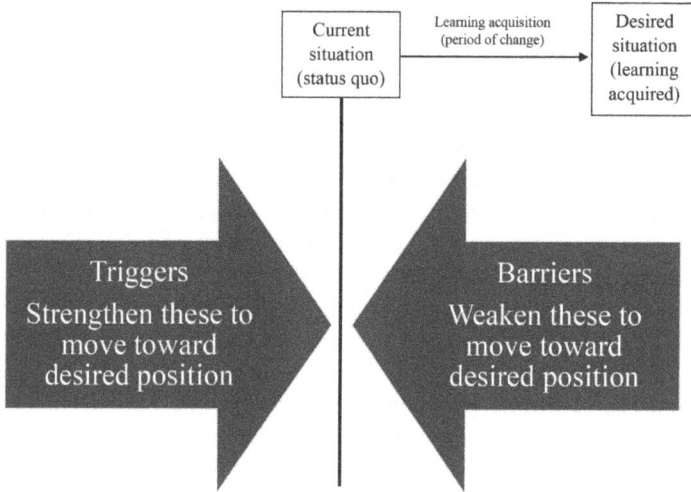

Source: Inspired by Lewin (1943).

Figure 6.1   Force-field analysis for change

Drawing from the force-field example, we can begin to identify some of the barriers to learning acquisition that I presented in Part I of the book. Key factors that you believe will emerge as barriers to change (e.g., low self-efficacy, fear of failure, struggles with forging an identity) need to be identified, and these should be recognized in the model as resisters, acting as forces working against the transition to a new state where learning has taken place.

While doing this you will also need to identify the factors that will facilitate learning (the antecedents of learning). These are the factors that help move the learner from the position of status quo by supporting their transition to the new state where learning has been acquired. As you can see in Figure 6.1, the factors that impede learning (barriers) need to be reduced or made weaker if the journey from the current situation to the desired one is to be accomplished satisfactorily and without too many challenges along the way. Similarly, you will need to strengthen the factors that will promote and support learning (the antecedents referred to above). This scenario is depicted in Figure 6.2, where examples of the reinforcers (triggers) and resisters (barriers) of learning have been identified.

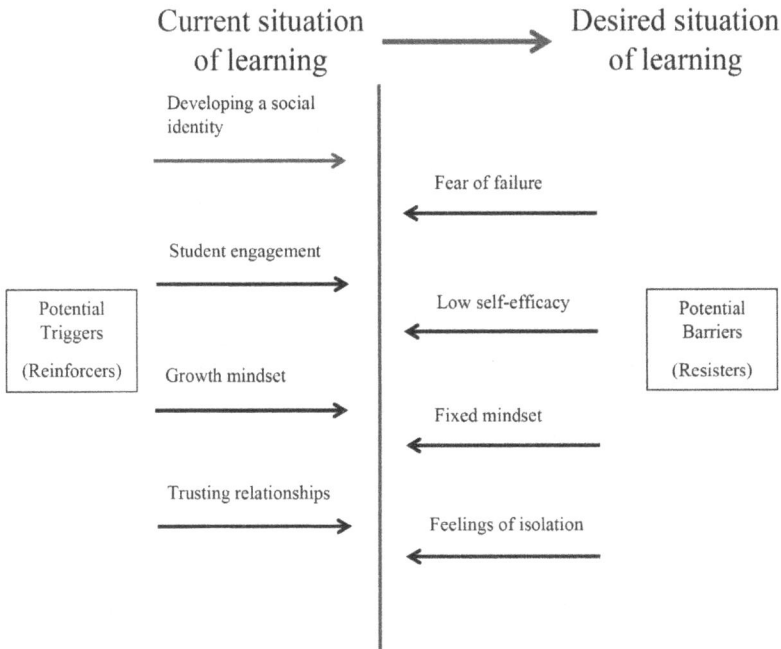

Current situation of learning → Desired situation of learning

Developing a social identity →

Fear of failure ←

Student engagement →

Potential Triggers (Reinforcers)

Low self-efficacy ←

Potential Barriers (Resisters)

Growth mindset →

Fixed mindset ←

Trusting relationships →

Feelings of isolation ←

Source: Inspired by Lewin (1943).

Figure 6.2   *Barriers and triggers to learning seen through the lens of force-field analysis*

Following this process should help to add a level of granularity and bring clarity to the initial stages of building your course. However, I would also advise returning to this model at regular intervals to reflect on how effectively you are managing the reinforcers and resisters and to consider if there are any tweaks you can make in future. Unless these barriers are checked, there is capacity for them to persist throughout the student's time at university, affecting the quality of their learning and their learning experience during that journey.

In this chapter I want to connect you with the theories of learning that promote a student-centered andragogical experience, one that encourages the student to place themselves at the forefront of their own learning while they still receive all the support they need to succeed. This student-centered approach to learning is aligned with the constructivist one as opposed to the more traditional tutor-centered approach (often referred to as instructivist). I will set out the reasons why it is better to be guided by the constructivist approach and how, by doing so, you will encourage your students to undertake a deeper form of learning. This account will also consider the barriers to learning we discussed in Part I and begin to give you some ideas about how to develop a toolkit to build your course and avoid some of the pitfalls to learning I have already discussed so far.

To provide some context for this discussion, let us begin by taking a closer look at the concepts of surface learning and deep learning.

6.2   APPROACHES TO LEARNING: SURFACE LEARNING AND DEEP LEARNING

It is appropriate to begin the conversation about constructivist and instructivist principles of course design by looking at their relationship with both the deep and surface approaches to learning. A third approach, strategic learning, where a central aim of the student is to learn what they need to know to maximize their marks on the course, tends to align more closely to surface learning in terms of its characteristics. In this section I want to focus on surface learning and deep learning approaches and the reasons why deep forms of learning need to be encouraged when your primary focus is andragogic development.

6.2.1   The Characteristics of Each Approach

The concept of deep and surface approaches to learning originated from research conducted by Marton and Säljö (1976). Surface learning is adopted by students who want to do enough to pass the course and therefore only learn what is essential. Surface forms of learning do not necessarily demonstrate a good understanding of the material being learned and are often associated with memory and rote learning, tending to be more conducive for short-term memory retention.

Deep forms are associated with the intrinsic benefits of learning and a universal engagement with the subject matter being learned. Sensemaking of the material being learned is essential, along with the ability to make connections between different strands or elements of the subject content. Deep learning involves interpreting the concepts being learned, committing them to long-term memory, and allowing learners to build knowledge on top of what they already know. The deep form of learning aligns with the constructivist approach, where a central tenet is to encourage the learner to willingly connect with the content and delivery of your course – another illustration of why it is so important for us to develop strategies that cultivate identity and deeper forms of engagement with the course delivery.

In relation to each approach to learning, Faranda et al. (2021) draw together some of the key strengths and weaknesses that have been highlighted across a range of studies over the years (Baeten et al., 2010; Ballantine et al., 2018; Byrne et al., 2002; Diseth, 2003, 2007; Entwhistle et al., 1979; Sun and Richardson, 2012). In their paper the comparison between surface and deep learning approaches draws attention to the difference in level of pedagogical development between the two. The chief motive of a student who adopts a surface learning approach is to avoid failing the course, whereas those students who engage in a deeper form of learning are recognized as possessing an intrinsic interest in the course learning matter. While outcomes in relation to the final grade for some assessments may be similar for both deep and surface learners (i.e., they will achieve their goals by obtaining a pass), deep learning allows the learner to go beyond outcomes purely focused on grades. A key aim of the deep learning methodology is to help the student develop a building-block approach to acquiring knowledge, aligning closely with the principles of the constructivist form of learning. Along with the outcomes and processes associated with each approach, Table 6.1 shows the main motives and intentions of the surface learner and deep learner as presented by Faranda et al. (2021) from their review of the research.

It is true that in some situations surface learning can also support knowledge development, particularly where time is limited and only a basic understanding and foundational knowledge of a subject is needed to perform a function or task. However, we are considering these learning approaches in the context of course delivery and it is assumed that there will be sufficient time incorporated to allow for a deep form of learning.

We can see from Table 6.1 that surface learning is recognized as a form of study without reflection or purpose and avoids the integration of different elements of the learning content. Inevitably, an unwillingness to engage with a deeper form of learning forgoes the opportunity to develop important skills, such as research, analysis, evaluation, and synthesis of theory and subject content. The inevitable impact of this is that when there is a need to draw on those skills next time, any students that did not partake in deep learning may well fall short again. A lack of engagement on your course could also result in learning and development being impeded at later stages of the program.

6.2.2 Designing to Dig Deep

When designing courses, one of our principal objectives should be to encourage students to develop a pattern of effective learning where they will need to

Table 6.1   *Motives, intentions, outcomes, and processes associated with students' approaches to learning*

Approach	Motive	Intention	Outcome and processes
Surface approach	Avoid failure	To reproduce	Outcome: incomplete understanding • Memorizing and rote learning for assessments • Balancing between working too hard and learning just enough to get through the task • Meeting course requirements with minimum effort • Studying without reflecting or purpose • Failing to differentiate concepts from practical application and examples • Treating tasks as external impositions • Focusing on tasks and discrete elements without integration
Deep approach	Intrinsic interest in the course subject matter	To understand	Outcome: extensive understanding • Actualizing interest and competence • Seeking meaning • Relating ideas to prior knowledge and everyday experiences • Comprehending the material presented • Engaging with course content • Collaborating with others • Examining logic • Using evidence and focusing on arguments • Committing to learn for personal reasons

Source: Adapted from Faranda et al. (2021, p. 11).

engage in a structured process of higher-order thinking – for instance, setting your students short tasks to complete during their independent learning time[1] that require problem solving, analysis, evaluation, or a form of reflective practice rather than, for example, relying on a reading assignment as a single form of prep for the next teaching session. In fact, an over-dependence on reading and consuming information is not necessarily conducive to deep forms of learning. A variety of short but analytical prep tasks that can be consolidated into a single point of learning and include a need to both understand and evaluate content are more helpful than a long reading task where non-visual-type learners may find it difficult to focus and can easily lose interest. Of course, this could also include a reading task where most appropriate.

Where reading to gather information is necessary, make sure there is an objective, such as to help in problem solving or finding solutions (i.e., there is a clear purpose). Managing the students' workload and allowing them more time to think deeply is what is required. Tasks that require students to evaluate and analyze course content rather than purely understand and reproduce information will encourage a deeper form of engagement.

I should also give assessment a brief mention at this point. Beyond the design of classroom activities, assessment in its various forms can have an impact on how students engage with both the content of your course and what you are asking them to do in pre-sessional, in-sessional, and post-sessional activities. Where the assessment tends to guide the student toward a strategy of surface learning (e.g., Multiple Choice Question (MCQ) test, standard closed-book exam) rather than the need for a deeper development of course knowledge, students are more likely to opt for strategies that include memorization of content through rote forms of learning when preparing for the assessment. To encourage a deeper form of learning, make sure that:

1. the marking scheme is made available for students to access early in the module;
2. it includes a wide range of criteria that will be used as a gauge to assess the students' work;
3. it builds in higher-order learning expectations and offers visibility of what students need to achieve for higher-level marks while learning is underway.

I have included an example of marking criteria for a group written report in Appendix 1.

6.2.3   Influence of the Learning Environment

Thus, through the design of our courses and the choice and design of our teaching methods and assessment, we can guide students toward a deeper form of learning. But factors that have an impact on student engagement and their motivation to learn are also influenced by the learning environment – for example, if students are finding the learning environment too challenging due to, let us say, the pace of course delivery, or the lack of support provided by the course leader and wider teaching team. Those students who still lack high-level skills in their evaluation of course content, such as the ability to analyze critically and apply reflective practice, may find they are unable to engage in the same way as other students around them. A likely outcome from this scenario is that they will feel at a disadvantage, and that they are beginning to fall behind.

An inclination to deep learn content may also be influenced by some of the other factors I discussed in Part I of the book that impact student confidence, such as self-efficacy, fear of failing, or inclusivity issues that leave the learner on the outside rather than being integral to the course learning environment. All these potential problems will increase the chance of disengaging with the course, making it much harder for the student to embrace a deep form of learning, opting instead to pursue a strategy of following the marks rather than a commitment to learning for personal reasons. Where this occurs, care needs to be taken. Disengagement evolving from a disconnect between the course objectives and a student's personal goals will quite probably discourage the higher level of integration with course content that is necessary for deep learning to take place.

Consequently, it is important to make clear to your students from the outset how the course content links with the course learning outcomes, and more generally with the wider program learning outcomes, and how the time they invest will feed into the bigger picture of achieving personal goals. It is important that students have clear visibility of how learning becomes the conduit that will help them to reach their own personal goals. These goals could range from the basics of achieving a good degree classification to more specific career goals that the student can clearly align with your course and its teaching content.[2]

In summary, deep forms of learning encourage more effective analysis through better engagement. Deep learning indicates the learner finds an intrinsic benefit from studying the brief and conducting research in a particular field, leading to a synthesis of information and more critical approaches to analysis and evaluation. It has been noted that students who choose a deep approach to learning often want to do so because they enjoy the intellectual challenges this imposes and the exploration of different interrelationships between concepts (Diseth, 2003, 2007; Sun and Richardson, 2012). Undoubtedly, a deeper form of learning fits closely with the constructivist learning paradigm, and so let us now take a closer look at constructivism.

6.3   APPROACHES TO LEARNING: CONSTRUCTIVISM

The central tenet of the constructivist approach to learning is that we seek new opportunities to build upon the foundations of previous learning, thus applying a building-blocks approach to knowledge development. Prerequisite knowledge, used to construct our knowledge base, is integrated with new learning experiences that help to build and develop knowledge at a higher level (Phillips, 1995). In this paradigm, learners learn by interacting with their environment, where there is an expectation that they will negotiate their own understanding of the situation (Pande and Bharathi, 2020). By undertaking a series of teaching activities that are developed around problem solving, learners will be expected to construct their own meaning (subjectivist learning). So, the constructivist way is a learner-active form of learning, offering an alternative mode to the more passive forms of tutor-led learning. In its purest form, the andragogic argument for constructivism is that knowledge should be individually constructed by the student as opposed to being transmitted by the tutor, recognizing that each learner's experience of learning will be unique (Van Bergen and Parsell, 2019).

At this stage it might be useful for me to set out the key principles of constructivism and compare these to the often-described contrasting paradigm of behaviorist learning theory. Aylward and Cronje (2022) recognize the constructivist paradigm as a world that is structured by individual processing of perceptions that are based on the nature of our interactions with it. The world as we see it is highly subjective and dependent on many antecedents, such as experience, cultural insights, our formative development, and a range of other individual differences. This active interaction with one's social world goes beyond passive forms of knowledge transmission where knowledge is typically communicated by the message sender and, instead, encourages the construction of new knowledge through the process of experience and social discourse. As you may expect, this form of knowledge development is context-dependent and contingent on the environment, social setting, and cultural experience of the learning event.

The behaviorist (or objectivist) view, on the other hand, recognizes a single truth where we all see the world from the same perspective; meaning is not subject-dependent but exists independently of the human mind. In this paradigm, reality is a perspective that can be commonly shared with others who will experience the same understanding. Meaning is controlled externally and not intrinsically derived.

Tutor-led forms of delivery can be important in some contexts and have a role in the process of learning. A good example to illustrate this is a situation where there needs to be consistency in the dissemination of information or new knowledge to a large group of students. A strength of using a more guided form of instruction, such as tutor-centered learning, is that knowledge is transferred intact and there is less opportunity for conflicting interpretations of meaning and different understandings by those receiving the information. Critics of the constructivist approach would argue that an absence of instructor-led teaching results in a less accurate form of knowledge dissemination due to an increased risk of misunderstandings arising from learner interpretation (Schweitzer and Stephenson, 2008). However, the challenges of successfully including interactive content within traditional instructor-led contexts means that this often remains a passive form of learning.

Thus, we see from the evidence that each of these two paradigms offers a quite distinct perspective of how knowledge is (and therefore should be) generated by the knowledge provider in their relationship with the learner. Depending on one's view, this may lead to a preference for either tutor-centered learning, aligning more with the behaviorist/objectivist paradigm of learning, or student-centered learning, aligning more with the constructivist/subjectivist paradigm of learning.

While it has been acknowledged that both perspectives have their strengths and weaknesses, an argument often touted to support the constructivist perspective is that tutor-centered learning, such as the traditional lecture, is not an effective way to engage students; this passive form of learning necessitates little or no conscious effort from the student (hence the reference to a passive form of learning). In the constructivist paradigm, a student needs to be actively engaged to learn effectively and engagement is more likely to be derived from a student-centered approach that demands them taking both control of (autonomous learning) and an enhanced level of responsibility for their own learning.

6.3.1   Acknowledging the Benefits and Limitations of Constructivist Learning

So, although there are benefits to be had from both the constructivist and instructivist paradigms of teaching, my central argument throughout this book highlights the greater opportunities arising in higher education from the adoption of a student-centered approach to course design. There is a strong belief that courses and programs where tutor-centered learning approaches still predominate no longer serve the various stakeholder needs and expectations of contemporary higher education – not least the broad skills-based offering that aligns more closely with the needs of graduate employers and students who want to leave higher education readily equipped for the demands they will encounter in their early careers. Increasingly, passive forms of learning do not fulfill the needs of graduate employers, who are looking for new recruits who not only come equipped with the necessary technical skills but are also equipped and career ready with the range of soft skills they will need for today's workplace.

The change in focus away from a command-and-control-style tutor-led model offered by traditional methods of teaching has, in part, been inspired by the increased availability of technological teaching aids that have encouraged fresh ideas about how to make learning more interactive and more inclusive. As I discussed in Part I of the book, both are key components of successful student engagement. But, even so, some elements of the instructivist model still have a place in the new order that is emerging in higher education, particularly in situations where direction and guidance is the principal objective.[3]

While a dual approach that accommodates an instructivist mode of teaching may still be necessary, moving to a student-centered (i.e., constructivist) model of teaching as early as possible on your course will deliver the benefits of a more active form of learning. This is one reason building student confidence, engagement, identity, and inclusivity early on is so important. Support for the constructivist approach to teaching in higher education is well documented.[4]

6.3.2 Adopting a Constructivist Approach

If one is to embrace and adopt a constructivist epistemology, then it is likely to involve some change to both teaching delivery and assessment. In some cases, the change may be quite radical. Where this is the case, you need to be particularly considerate of new students who will be at the start of their university journey. For this group of students, the change to the learning environment when compared to a previous environment more dependent on instruction and guidance may mean they need some time to adjust to a different approach to learning. In these cases, it may be necessary at the very outset of your course to adopt a mixed approach that involves a blend of instructivist learning (tutor-centered) and constructivist learning (student-centered). I say this with caution, because if you want to adopt a constructivist teaching approach then, as students grow in confidence and begin to manage more of their own learning, there needs to be a speedy transition for the tutor from a role of instructor to the role of facilitator.

As you make this transition, the high level of interactive social discourse that is encouraged by constructivist forms of learning can easily be incorporated into activities within the classroom – for example, lots of group-based working in seminar- or workshop-style learning environments. But if you genuinely want to adopt a more constructivist model of learning for your course then from an early stage you should also encourage students to extend this intensity of engagement outside of the tutor-facilitated classroom through the development of peer-to-peer learning and small study support groups. Importantly, Hailikari et al. (2022) have noted that a deeper form of learning can be promoted by group work through the process of peer support by 'sharing and constructing knowledge together' (p. 225).

If you include group projects or assignments on your course, then students should be naturally inclined to instigate and manage their own small study groups. If you do not already have a group summative assessment on your course, then you could consider designing a formative assessment for student groups instead. In addition, you can encourage students to interact and work together online by setting up a discussion board and/or small group discussion spaces in your learning management system.

The greater autonomy offered by this student-centered form of learning will encourage students to embrace a more active and dynamic approach. Suddenly, they are problem solving and producing solutions together, recognizing their peers as a valuable source of learning by way of sharing knowledge through the process of group interaction and rumination. This form of peer and group learning experience can also help to improve motivation and, through a more interactive learning style, self-efficacy and confidence. There is also the potential benefit of bringing people into the learning circle who would otherwise be reticent about joining in, thereby promoting inclusivity of minority groups while also helping to affirm understanding for those struggling to make sense of complex material – thus addressing some of the student-related issues I outlined in Part I of the book.

6.3.2.1 Reflection and self-assessment

Making reflection a core element of a student's learning journey is a key principle of a constructivist-centric learning culture and a pathway that I would encourage you to support. There are several ways of introducing reflective practice to your students. This can be as straightforward as asking them to create and maintain a journal that they can complete and refer to during their learning journey. Or you could incorporate reflection into assessment, setting a reflective assignment as either a formative or summative element of the assessment.

If you are thinking about including reflection in the design of a formative assessment, you could consider using either peer- or self-evaluation as at least part fulfillment of the assessment. This is yet another example of how the student can take more responsibility for their own work, enabling a better-integrated approach to learning that connects the learner with peers who will be traveling along the same journey. While a peer can offer a student a comparable benchmark to their own work, peer-assessed forms of feedback can be used to complement the generic feedback and marking guidance that you will also offer the group. Students can then be encouraged to use the generic form of marking guidance to self-assess their work.

The move toward a more student-centered approach will be dependent on you successfully encouraging the students to take responsibility for a significant element of their own learning while being supported and facilitated all the way along that learning journey by the course tutors. In many cases this may mean a change in behavior from the students' previous experiences in education. A move to encourage both self- and peer evaluation for some, or all, of the formative assessment supports the development of a constructivist learning strategy, encouraging the shift to a more responsible and self-autonomous learning environment. This is particularly important as the student moves from a highly structured and directed form of learning in high school or college to the university learning environment where achievement will become synonymous with those who successfully embrace independent forms of learning.

Having made the case for constructivist epistemology, I now move on to explain how you might embed this into your teaching using the framework of constructive alignment – the alignment of learning outcomes, teaching methods, and forms of assessment.

6.4 APPROACHES TO LEARNING: THE CONCEPT OF CONSTRUCTIVE ALIGNMENT

Constructive alignment theory (CAT) was initially proffered by Biggs (1996) as an approach to designing course content and delivery through the configuration of the course's learning outcomes, teaching and learning activities, and methods of assessment. The principles of the theory are quite straightforward: a student's level of attainment is dependent on how well they achieve in relation to each of the course's learning outcomes. This relationship between the learning outcomes and evaluating the student's proficiency of learning in relation to each of those learning outcomes is captured in the method of summative assessment used for your course. The philosophical ideology that underpins this approach is constructivism. Teaching is student-centered (as opposed to tutor-centered), adopting an active learning approach where tutors assume more of a learning facilitator role. Student learning outcomes are therefore central to instructional design in the form of teaching and learning activities, and central to all forms of course assessment.

The third element of this relationship highlights the importance of the methods used to deliver the course (the course learning activities), helping to actuate the learning outcomes and prepare the students for any formative and/ or summative course assessment. The theory is depicted in Figure 6.3 and, as you will note, the three elements are mutually dependent.

The 'constructive' element of the theory relates to 'the idea that students construct meaning through relevant learning activities. That is, meaning is not something imparted or transmitted from teacher to learner but is something learners have to create for themselves' (Biggs, 2003, p. 1). The 'alignment' element of the theory 'refers to what the teacher does, which is to set up a learning environment that supports the learning activities appropriate to achieving the desired learning outcomes' (Biggs, 2003, p. 1).

Many studies point toward the improved results in terms of both the quality of the course and student outcomes when constructive alignment is actively engaged in the course design (see for example Wang et al., 2013; Treleaven and Voola, 2008; Harvey and Kamvounias, 2008; Sumsion and Goodfellow, 2004; Larkin and Richardson, 2013). Let us look more closely at the concept of constructive alignment.

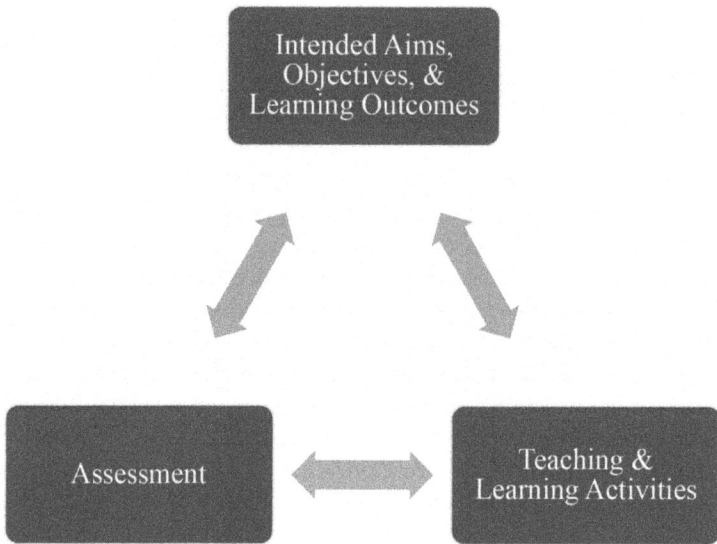

Source: Biggs (1996).

Figure 6.3   The constructive alignment of higher education courses

6.4.1   Aligning Your Course Constructively

In the constructive alignment approach to design, the intended learning outcomes become central to everything from the course structure to the teaching methods and activities and the forms of assessment. Attending to more basic learning outcomes centered around knowledge development and understanding will not necessarily need the same level of learning activities as more complex ones, such as problem solving, analysis, and evaluation skills.

While course aims and objectives can be left more open and generic, learning outcomes need to be specific and make a clear statement setting out the additional knowledge the student should be able to take away with them upon completion of the course. For clarity, they are best presented in bullet point format, and while they will be informed primarily by your course learning aims and objectives, they should also be guided by the objectives and learning outcomes of the program in which your course is situated.

These principles are also relevant if you are a program director and either redesigning your program or developing a new one. Although program learning objectives and learning outcomes tend to be more generic than those based on specific content at course level, the principles of development are the same.

Bearing in mind the program objectives and learning outcomes will also form a guiding light for your course leaders during their course design phase, your ambition should be to set a standard and develop a starting point to help inform course leaders when they are establishing their own course aims, objectives, and learning outcomes.

To begin your statement of intent for course design, you should start with an overall summary, setting out in more general terms the content of your course and what you want your students to learn. Here you can present the nature of the subject matter and anything you feel is important for the student to be aware of in advance of the course starting, such as any technical content that will be covered (e.g., basic accounting principles, or how to develop financial statements) or, perhaps, any content that you will be delivering through a series of lab simulations.

The content included in the course summary section should provide a more general outline, but aimed at offering the student enough information to decide whether the course content is suitable for them and, importantly, whether they believe the skills they will learn are conducive to their learning goals. It is important to note that some skills, such as group-working skills or interpersonal skills, may be difficult to assess directly, and so these could be identified in a separate sub-section as transferable skills, rather than including them as course learning outcomes. It is not expected that these transferable skills will be directly assessed, but they will nevertheless form an important aspect of your intended learning journey for the student. Of course, the learning outcomes will need to be evaluated at some point via summative assessment.

Following the development of the course summary, the next section should include the learning aims and objectives, which can be developed as a short paragraph providing an outline of what the course intends to help the student achieve by the time it is complete. This may include similar content to the course summary and so, as an alternative, you could consider combining the two sections.

Moving on now to the learning outcomes, as previously mentioned, these are best presented in a bullet point format, which will enhance visibility and provide a summary checklist for students before and after they have completed the course. It will also offer you a helpful checklist once your course is ready to run each year. I suggest aiming to develop between 3–6 learning outcomes, depending on how long your course lasts and how much content you intend to cover. Subject to how detailed the learning outcome section is, you may also wish to include some skills that are easily observed and that you are able to assess. However, bear in mind that whatever you include in the learning outcome section will need to be formally assessed at some point.

As alluded to earlier, other skills that you are not able to directly assess can be included in a separate section entitled Transferable Skills. Although forming an important part of the intended course learning, because they are not directly assessable, these skills will not be included with other intended learning outcomes in the 'Learning Outcomes' section. If course catalogs are made available to students, it is likely that the students will want to observe key information, including the learning outcomes and any additional skills that are central to learning on the course. More generally, this will enable students to identify courses that can help them cultivate skills and close skills gaps that may be seen as essential for future career prospects. This will be particularly helpful if your course is available as an option to them and where students need to research information about a range of courses that may be of interest to them before selecting your course to become part of their formal program.

As an example, Box 6.1 shows the element of a course inventory or catalog entry that includes each of the sections I refer to above, and may be helpful as a template when designing your own course.

BOX 6.1   A TRUNCATED COURSE INVENTORY
OR CATALOG ENTRY DEMONSTRATING
THE COURSE SUMMARY, AIMS AND
OBJECTIVES, LEARNING OUTCOMES,
AND TRANSFERABLE SKILLS

Course Summary

This course presents and evaluates current knowledge about human behavior in organizations from the point of view of the individual employee, the work group, and the organization itself. There is an emphasis on developing relevant skills through learning theoretical content and following this up with the practical application of ideas in a management context. A critical perspective is adopted throughout.

Indicative content: The course introduces the key concepts, theories, and research in the field of Organizational Behavior, and demonstrates their practical relevance for management. This involves an examination of:

*   how the discipline has developed in relation to changing management practices from the early 20th century;
*   personality, individual differences, learning and motivation;
*   managing groups and teams, the influence of the 'social organization,' and workplace cultures;
*   leadership, power and politics, managing change, the impact of technology and from globalization.

This is all presented within the context of social responsibility and workforce diversity.

Learning Aims and Objectives

The course aims to provide students with knowledge of the different levels of behavior established in the workplace (i.e., individual, group, and organization level). In doing so, the student will be able to better understand the manager's role in a contemporary organization. In addition, the course aims to equip the student with sufficient knowledge to be able to recognize the influence on organizational outcomes from a range of employee attitudes and behaviors.

Learning Outcomes

On completion of this course, students will be able to:

- Identify and describe the relationship between organizational behavior and management practice.
- Critically analyze competing theoretical perspectives on organizational behavior.
- Comprehend and analyze appropriate source material for academic writing.
- Demonstrate an understanding of the key theoretical perspectives of managing employee behavior.
- Display good academic writing skills, including citation, referencing, structure, academic report writing, and application of critical awareness.

Transferable Skills

In addition to the course learning outcomes, the course is designed to help students develop the following skills, transferable to other environments:

- interpersonal skills
- interactive group-working skills
- leadership
- problem solving
- debating and negotiation skills
- presentation skills.

Once you have developed this information the next step is to consider how the course would be best delivered to students (e.g., a series of lectures, workshops, and/or seminars supported by digital tools available in an online workspace). How it will be delivered may be dictated by the window of time that is open to you (i.e., whether it will be delivered as an intensive course over a short period of a few days or a longer course over a period of either terms or semesters). This may also be a suitable time to return to the learning barriers discussed in Part I of the book and that I set out in the framework presented in Figure 6.2. Recognizing potential learning barriers and making early decisions on how these can be managed through course design (i.e., through the design of your teaching and learning activities) is another way you can support students to achieve their learning goals.

The development of the course learning aims/objectives and outcomes, the creation of the delivery structure, and the designing of support tools for students to use will be an iterative process as you work your way through the design stage. Some things will seem to make sense from the outset but will need to be forfeited as you realize that you cannot achieve everything in a single course.

The final link in the design chain is developing the methods of assessment. This should be a logical step once you have decided what you want your students to achieve and have identified the methods you want to use to deliver your course. However, it is no less an important part of this process. You may have got the first two stages right, but if your methods of assessing the students are not reliable and valid then it will be almost impossible to judge how successful you have been in achieving your course aims. Even more importantly, students will not have an accurate record of their own achievement on your course. The final mark is important to them, but of equal importance is the opportunity for them to reflect and consider how they can apply their learning from the outcomes of any assessment to feed forward into their next one.

In Chapter 7 I will go on to consider and discuss individually and in more detail each of the three phases of constructive alignment in course design.

6.5   CHAPTER SUMMARY

In the first chapter of Part II my ambition has been to define a context from which you can begin to envision your own course design. In doing so, I have pursued the constructivist concept, setting out with justification why this approach is right for the contemporary higher education climate. By extolling the virtues of deep learning in comparison with surface learning you can see how the central principles of constructivist student-centered andragogy are better placed to offer more efficient and effective forms of outcome to student learning. I have also set out the benefits and limitations of the constructivist approach, which will help you to identify if there are aspects of your course delivery that require a more tutor-centered approach to learning so that you can make appropriate choices in the design stage.

Building on the constructivist concept of learning, I also introduced the framework of constructive alignment. The framework proposes that students should be encouraged to construct their own meaning of each learning event. The constructive alignment approach also proposes that a close alignment of the learning outcomes, learning activities, and course assessment is key to effective course design. More generally, understanding the objectives of a constructivist student-centered teaching approach and how this will support an ambition to encourage your students to partake in deeper forms of learning is important for building a strategy. Developing the course framework is the starting point, and once you have this, filling in the details can follow.

The detail is what I go on to identify in Chapter 7 when I discuss at length the design of a constructively aligned course, beginning with the construction of the aims, objectives, learning outcomes, and transferable skills. Building on these, I discuss the development of learning and teaching activities, followed by the methods of assessment.

NOTES

1. In referring to the students' 'independent learning time' I am talking about the time the student allocates outside of their core teaching to work on course-related tasks that may have been set for them by their tutor, or, for example, for extended reading and other forms of data gathering. The amount of independent learning time that a student is expected to dedicate to their overall course learning should be clearly presented in the course catalog alongside the number of teaching hours that are dedicated to the course.
2. It is important that each student is encouraged to develop a series of personal goals soon after they arrive at university. These could be short term (e.g., annual), focused more on the medium term (end of the student's program), or longer term (a five-year plan that includes the student's early career objectives), or even a combination of each. Essentially, these will be discussed and developed in one-to-one personal tutor meetings and/or encouraged during the students' professional development course.
3. For example, at the outset of a new course or during the early days of a new project where learners will need the certainty offered through tutor instruction.
4. Van Bergen and Parsell (2019) provide examples.

7. Course design: the triadic interactive framework of constructive alignment

7.1 INTRODUCTION

In Chapter 6 I set out a framework for course design that encourages you to embrace a more active student-centered model of learning while moving away from tutor-centered forms of teaching delivery and assessment. The central aim is to engage your students with a deeper form of learning that will offer them a more fulfilling experience during their time on your course. The move toward a student-centered approach to learning can help your students gain confidence while enabling them to become better all-round independent learners.

In the last section of Chapter 6 I introduced you to the framework of constructive alignment, an approach to course design that is inspired by and cognizant of the constructivist concept of learning. In this chapter I will provide a more detailed account of the principles of constructive alignment and outline the process you will need to follow to adopt the framework for your course.

7.2 IT'S ALL ABOUT AIMS, OBJECTIVES, AND LEARNING OUTCOMES

Establishing the intended learning outcomes (ILOs) is a key priority of early course design and is an activity that should form part of an iterative process with the development of the course aims and objectives. In effect, everything that is shaped within the design stage – the course structure, subject content, range of intellectual and practical skills, types of assessment and what you will want to assess – will all be informed by the ILOs, aims, and objectives. The course learning outcomes perform a similar function to the research questions or hypotheses of an empirical study; their function is to operationalize what you aim to achieve. Whereas the aims and objectives are usually visible through the design of your course, the learning outcomes are often unseen and so will need to be formally assessed to provide evidence that they have been achieved.

Thurner and Böttcher (2022) maintain that the relationship between ILOs and the planned teaching and learning activities will be dependent on the goals you set for your course, which, in turn, will help inform the teaching methods you intend to use. So, once you have been able to structure your aims and objectives, and define the learning outcomes, you are ready for the next stage, which is to consider the most appropriate methods of delivery. This will include considering the range of media or tools at your disposal that could be used to transmit the delivery (e.g., in-person delivery v. online interactive tools).

Although constructive alignment has been exemplified and debated by many in relation to course design, there has been much less recognition of the student-profile factors that I discussed in Part I of this book, such as confidence, engagement, and identity. I want to return your thoughts to these factors and then consider how they can be integrated in a course designed under the auspices of constructive alignment. While these factors are unlikely to feature as ILOs, they will be critical to the successful functioning of your course and to the motivations of the students you are trying to inspire to successfully meet those learning outcomes.

7.2.1 Type of Learning Outcome: Intellectual Skills and Practical Skills

While there are a range of factors that could help shape your course learning outcomes, inevitably these factors will be dependent on what you are trying to achieve (i.e., the central aims of your course and the learning goals). For example, is a central aim to develop specific skills? If so, the focus may be to pitch your learning outcomes toward more practical elements of the course rather than the intellectual content. It is also possible that your course learning outcomes will be associated with the next level of study. If so, prerequisite learning could also become a consideration.[1]

It is helpful to think of ILOs in terms of targets that you want to set for your students. If the target is too ambitious, then many students will fail to achieve your level of expectation, in which case it could impact their confidence before they move on to the next level of study. So, from the outset, it is essential that you are realistic about what you can expect from the cohort of students (i.e., knowing the cohort you will be delivering to), rather than having overly ambitious aspirations about what they could achieve. This may be dependent on your cohort's prior learning, which might vary depending on the diversity of the group and their previous experience in relation to the subject matter you will be teaching.

As I previously mentioned, the early design phase is an iterative process, and so while the course goals (aims and objectives) will help to inform the

ILOs, in turn the ILOs will also help to shape, refine, and adapt the course goals you want to achieve. This reciprocal and interactive process between the development of the ILOs and the development of the goals should be considered part of ongoing continuous improvement and included in any post-course reflection. It could also be informed by any student feedback you are able to glean (e.g., course evaluation) and be used to make changes as necessary to strengthen aspects of the design for future delivery.

7.3   METHODS OF DELIVERY

Contextualizing the design of your course through the development of its aims, its objectives, and the learning outcomes is critical as the first step. However, once you are satisfied with your ILOs the logical order of things means it is time to move on to give some thoughtful consideration to the most appropriate and effective ways to deliver your course content and thereby give your students a chance to achieve those learning outcomes. In doing so, this will be a good point once again to revisit some of the factors identified in Part I of the book that could impact a student's readiness to learn (e.g., engaging students, helping them to form identities, building their self-confidence, and feeling included).

   How we design our teaching is one of the key factors that determine how students behave and approach learning. High-quality teaching materials and methods of delivery that challenge students are far more likely to encourage active participation, both inside and outside the classroom. Higher levels of student participation will help to promote better interaction with their peers, and that sharing of knowledge I discussed earlier through a culture of peer support and through student-centered learning. While tutor-centered learning methods can still make a valuable contribution toward overall effective teaching delivery, passive forms of learning do not necessarily encourage the deeper forms of learning behavior that you want to instill in your students, such as analysis and reflection. These forms of learning behavior will respond better to a more active, student-centered approach.

7.3.1   Learning to Teach while Teaching to Learn

Starting course design (or redesign) from scratch offers an opportunity for you to revisit your modes of teaching and delivery and be more radical in your approach, although you also need to be cautious that you do not end up throwing out the baby with the bath water. It is essential that you understand what has worked well for you and your students over time because, while it is important to look forward, it is of equal importance to be able to look back. For example, the period during the Covid pandemic made us see our life in teaching through a new lens as we adapted to survive, even though, on occasion, some of our best attempts to engage students using technology to deliver synchronous teaching almost died on their feet. While we accept that this was the case in some of our worst experiences during the crisis, when we were able to return to a life that we were more familiar with pre-pandemic, this did not necessarily mean the new methods of delivery were rejected out of hand. On the contrary, some of the digital learning activities that we adapted to and adopted during the pandemic helped us to improve the range of andragogical activity, and the overall quality of our delivery to students.

For many of us in teaching at that time, when we switched to digital forms of delivery the learning trajectory was very steep. One outcome of this as we made our way back onto campus was that the quality and engagement with digital delivery was enhanced exponentially when compared to our dalliances with it pre-Covid. The result is that universities have become much more proficient at multi-mode teaching delivery that includes a mix of what works well from digital delivery with more traditional forms of in-person activity. What many of us have found is that the less interactive aspects of our teaching, including students preparing work for in-person classes, and content that was previously delivered in large group sessions in the format of a traditional lecture, work very well in digital format where students can be directed to access it with some flexibility over a given timescale. With adequate structure through appropriate guidance and support, this can offer students more autonomy over their learning.[2]

Now, I am not saying that this does not present its own challenges, and you will not please everyone with your chosen methods of delivery. For 'flexibility and autonomous learning' for some students, read 'lack of structure and direction' for others. However, as we have moved toward a more blended form of teaching delivery, the general impression I have gleaned from my colleagues and others I have spoken to from within the realms of higher education teaching is that most students have found the additional flexibility and increased autonomy in their learning to be a positive step. It also allows you to distinguish between distinct levels of interaction. So, for example, retaining content delivery that works better with high levels of interaction for the in-person sessions, and designing lower-interactive medium including asynchronous video and online forums for situations where interaction is typically very low or non-existent.[3]

You will learn to know what works best for you and your students. However, we should not assume that students will only appreciate our course if we are seen to be applying the latest forms of technology and digital learning. Students thrive in a learning environment that increases understanding, adds clarity to expectations, eliminates uncertainty, and allows for an interactive experience in a safe space. It may be that you are much better at delivering this to your students by adopting an in-person teaching delivery that is more tutor-centered but still considers many of the critical factors we discussed in Part I of the book. Just because it appears to work well for others does not necessarily mean it is the correct modus operandi for your course.

7.3.2   Collaborative Learning

Students learn best when they can work together and share their knowledge, which is why I tend to organize my teaching activities so that solutions are only possible through the exercise of collaborative problem solving. The benefits are numerous. For one, I am not left with a class full of students sitting in silence! But the main benefit is that it stimulates peer interaction, which has been found to play a key role in learning (e.g., see Yazici, 2004). It encourages active learning through the necessity for students to collaborate and engage with their peer group, personalizing their learning through that social context. The support a student receives from their group members can also reduce the likelihood of them giving up in the face of adversity when dealing with complex and challenging issues. Importantly, when students are given the opportunity to discuss a task while feeling safe within a small-group setting, support on this level has also been found to improve problem-solving and other cognitive skills such as interpretation and analysis.

The process of conversing within small groups enables the student to discuss the concept or issue under observation, helping to promote clarity and understanding of the concept and, if appropriate, requirements of the task the student has been set. A small-group setting helps to overcome potential issues with inclusivity, helping to bring in students who lack confidence speaking openly in larger-group settings, and may assist international students to overcome misunderstandings with language translation borne from purely tutor-led discussions. Cohen (1994) found that students are more likely to discuss content involving more complex and technical issues in accessible and amenable language, helping them to communicate issues and improve understanding of any complexity that may arise. Interestingly, Neer (1987) found that when students developed anxieties about public speaking, being able to discuss the subject matter first in small peer groups helped alleviate some of those anxieties.

Small-group activities offer an opportunity for the tutor(s) to move around within the teaching session and join up with each of the student groups as they work on the activity. This enables the tutor(s) to interact with their students in a much more intimate setting. Again, this can help improve clarity by eliminating any misunderstandings within the group about the task they have been set. Students who lack the confidence at this stage to participate in larger-group discussions or find some of the language barriers challenging[4] are likely to feel more comfortable speaking to the tutor in a more intimate small-group setting (i.e., consisting of 4–5 students). So, this can be an effective method of increasing participation and inclusivity for minority groups.

More generally, collaborative learning in small groups promotes inter-dependence between group members, particularly if this involves a task where there is high importance to the outcome.[5] Interdependence through collaboration promotes the trust-building process and encourages individual accountability (Cohen et al., 2017). In addition to helping with sensemaking, working regularly in small groups helps to develop the collaborative processes of mutual consensus-based decision-making and constructive peer review and feedback, which inevitably involves the experience of reflective practice.

Summing up this section, it would be simplistic to think that a successful design or redesign of your course will be limited to introducing new methods of teaching. Getting the foundations right is of equal importance and if one feels there is a reason to change the methods of teaching and learning activities, then it is possible that there also needs to be a review of the course aims, the learning outcomes, and the andragogic goals you wish to achieve. While it is important to try and develop the course around what we think students will find engaging and interesting, any changes need to be closely aligned to the learning outcomes and goals while at the same time being conscious of the barriers to student learning identified in Part I of this book. This could involve a shift out of your comfort zone as you try new ways of delivery that seek to apply constructive forms of learning rather than relying on the more traditional instructive, tutor-centered methods of learning that you may have grown used to.

7.4   ASSESSMENT

While it is often acknowledged that a continuous improvement of quality and standards requires a regular review and update of teaching practices, we are less inclined to update our modes of assessment (Boud et al., 2018). A constructive alignment framework acknowledges the impact of assessment and the level of influence it can have in guiding and shaping the behavior of students. Drawing on their own study findings, Cain et al. (2018) advise that assessment should be used in alignment with a constructivist teaching approach to help shape student learning.

7.4.1   ILOs and LOA

A constructive alignment approach to course design recognizes the central relationship between course learning outcomes and assessment design. This model of learning has become known as outcome-based education and is different from the traditional models of learning that are often based around the curriculum (Ibrahim et al., 2022). In the constructive alignment framework of course design the intended learning outcomes (ILOs) are used to guide the development of both the course content and assessment. Besides guiding students toward what they should be aiming to achieve from the course, this will also help students make sense of the way their course is structured, and why their assessment has been designed accordingly. It also increases the level of visibility for other interested stakeholders, such as employers, who will be interested in the alignment of your course with the development of skills. In the constructive alignment model, assessment is developed to provide an indicator of how well each student has performed in relation to each learning outcome. Where there is underachievement across the cohort of students, adjustments should be made to the course teaching and learning activities ensuring remedial action is applied to iron out any deficiencies.

Designing a course around its ILOs also offers the advantage of a more targeted approach to evaluating the effectiveness of learning that has taken place. It will also help you to evaluate the meeting of specific criteria that link directly back to the course aims and objectives via the course's ILOs. It also offers the opportunity for an evidence-based approach to measuring both the effectiveness and efficiency of teaching during course delivery (Ibrahim et al., 2022). This can be achieved on an ongoing basis by adopting suitable formative assessment activities, which should provide indicators that inform if adjustments to teaching delivery need to be made before outcomes are formally assessed in the course summative assessment, thereby developing an effective learning outcomes assessment approach through a combination of results from both the formative and summative assessment.

This is highlighted in Ibrahim et al.'s (2022) paper, which sets out the process of the learning outcomes assessment (LOA) model (outcomes-based education) that aims to encourage a continuous improvement narrative and encapsulates the three elements of constructive alignment. Ibrahim et al. (2022) propose that course leaders need to be asking the following series of questions to ensure that the LOA model is working both effectively and efficiently and that a continuous improvement loop is being applied:

- Are students achieving the intended outcomes?
- Are they gaining the required skills to succeed in their field or profession?
- Is the program continuously improving the student learning experience?
- Should the offered curriculum or the teaching pedagogies be modified?
- Are there other techniques or additional resources that would help students learn more effectively?

7.4.2   The Role of Formative Assessment

The value of formative assessment is often misrepresented by course leaders and misunderstood by some students who go on to dismiss it because they believe it will not contribute to their final mark and, hence, appears to have no observable benefit. But does it? There is a need to understand the important contributions from a formative assessment that has been designed to support successful achievement of the course aims and learning outcomes.

Formative assessment is seen as a way of giving feedback to students about their level of attainment at a particular point in the course. It can be designed purely as a standalone assessment that serves as an indicator of learning up to that point. In this form the course leader can also use it to highlight sections of the course that need further attention. Alternatively, formative assessment can be linked to one of the course summative assessments and deployed to provide feedback that is utilized as feedforward, highlighting where there are knowledge gaps in particular areas of the course syllabus. It may also function as a reliable barometer of where the student is currently heading in relation to the summative assessment, offering an indication of what and by how much they need to improve to achieve a good or better standard in the final reckoning.

One word of caution: where an indicative mark is also offered there is a risk that a student will place more emphasis on this than the feedback they have received. The benefit of including marks or indicative grades on formative assessment feedback has been called into doubt by some (e.g., Black and Wiliam, 1998; Skinner, 2014). The doubters here state that, where they are awarded, more emphasis is placed on the marks than on engaging usefully with the written advice as a valuable source of feedback. From a student's point of view, the feedback can be misunderstood as a way for the reviewer to justify the mark given rather than its intended purpose of providing feedforward. Even so, in cases where a mark is not offered it will beg questions from the student about how they can apply a value to their work.

If you would prefer not to award a specific mark, then a viable alternative is to suggest what grade boundary it would fall into and how much effort the student still needs to exert if they wish to improve their standard and reach a higher plateau. Coupled with the qualitative feedback, if they so wish, students can develop their own plan of improvement, identifying where the attention needs to be focused (e.g., 'my feedback states that I am on track to achieve a low 2:1 and so I need to improve in these specific areas so I can achieve a 1st').

Formative assessment can provide encouragement and acts as an indicator of the student's performance to date. Encouragement in this form can be used to build self-efficacy and to overcome the fear of failure. It can also be used to encourage greater engagement from students by highlighting the areas of learning where they can improve. Students are more likely to engage with the formative task if they can see a direct link with the summative assessment that they will be undertaking a bit later in the course.

7.4.3   Assessment Criteria

Once specific details about the assessment have been released to students it is quite commonplace for some of them to begin asking about how they will be assessed and what they will need to do to achieve a good mark. Some academics may feel uncomfortable releasing the assessment criteria to students, but doing so will help to reduce uncertainty while increasing equity, fairness, and transparency at a time that may well be quite stressful for them. Even so, you need to be aware that by making assessment criteria visible to students it may encourage them to focus only on the elements of the course that will be included in the marking scheme and ignore other elements that appear to fall outside. Norton (2004) raises the point that this can become a particular problem where specific content of the course is linked directly to the marking criteria, which can result in a student's almost formulaic attachment to this element of your course. Where this could occur, keeping the assessment criteria that you release to students as generic as possible will discourage them from adopting a more strategic game-playing approach to learning by avoiding areas of the course syllabus they feel will not be directly assessed.

Calls to provide more precise definitions of expectations and examples of how to meet these in the assessed work tend to increase as the assessment deadline approaches. In relation to the specific criteria relating to 'range of sources used' or 'evidence of research in the field,' I am constantly being asked 'how many references do I need to use in support of my essay?' This formulaic approach to developing an essay is not good practice and indicates that a template exists for how the essay should be written. This is one of the problems that emerges when offering students a previous example of a good attempt at the assessment. Providing such an example does not necessarily always lead to good practice being followed.

One way of avoiding this is to make the criteria more meaningful in relation to the course objectives by linking them directly to the course learning outcomes. As you will now be familiar with, the key principle of constructive alignment theory is that learning outcomes become the primary informer of both the course teaching and learning activities and how the course will be assessed. Aligning the assessment criteria closely to the course learning outcomes also clearly confirms that you are assessing the knowledge and skills specified in the course prospectus, helping your students make sense of the way they are being assessed.

This approach will also appeal to the interests of potential graduate employers and other practitioners who have an interest in the students' education and skills development. Employers want to see an obvious relationship between the skills you identify as learning outcomes, their recognition in the course assessment, and the level of attainment expected of each student. Graduate employers are going to be more interested in the range of skills their potential new appointments possess, including the employability skills and soft skills that can become readily transferable between different domains. So, you will be supporting your students' graduate ambitions by closely aligning your course assessment criteria with a tangible set of skills that are of key interest to graduate employers.

7.4.4   Peer Assessment

When used as formative evaluation with proper tutor facilitation, peer assessment follows the principles of constructive learning. It satisfies some of the key principles of the constructivist approach by promoting collaborative learning in groups and because it requires the learner to engage more with the process of self-assessment and self-regulation (Nicol et al., 2014; Reinholz, 2016). It also encourages the student to be reflective as they assess and compare the work of their peers with their own, supporting a more active approach to developing vital skills such as critical thinking, good referencing technique, and analysis and evaluation. An opportunity to assess someone else's attempt at the same piece of work can help to make sense of the task and broaden perspectives on different approaches to meeting the requirements of the task. Also, it encourages the student to take responsibility and adopt a more autonomous way of working, where they take more control over their own learning.

There are some issues to be managed with peer assessment, including the expertise of the student as an assessor and the potential inconsistency of skills across the group of student assessors (Liu and Carless, 2006). Where expertise is low, levels of tutor monitoring can be adjusted to provide the amount of support that is required. In any case, the tutor will need to facilitate particular aspects, such as making available the assessment criteria, clarifying expectations, and ensuring understanding of key terminology. It is acknowledged by Rico-Juan et al. (2022) that any issues with student expertise can be overcome by tutor guidance and student training throughout the peer assessment process. If treated as a learning exercise for students, then the appropriate level of initial support that is offered by the tutor should be considered in the same vein as any other learning exercise that the students are asked to undertake.

7.5   PRE-DELIVERY WORK: DEVELOPING THE COURSE AIMS, OBJECTIVES, AND LEARNING OUTCOMES

In Chapter 8 I will move on to discuss the practical aspects of course design in detail, setting out a three-phase plan for doing so. Before we get there, I want to highlight the pre-delivery planning work that will need to be undertaken to set out the context and framework for your course design.

In the early part of this chapter I emphasized the importance of being clear from the outset about what you want to achieve from your course (the aims and objectives) and how this aligns with the academic learning outcomes and other transferable skills. Time spent on developing or adapting these foundation stones will help to refine and clarify what you need to focus on when designing your course (i.e., the content, delivery structure, and approaches to assessment).

Following the principles of constructive alignment, you must also decide how you are going to assess the students at this point, setting out a detailed plan of what this will look like. It will mean setting out detailed assessment criteria where each criterion clearly aligns with one or more of your ILOs, recognizing what the student will need to do to be successful at each level of the grading system. This will usually require being able to distinguish between different levels of achievement depending on what your grading system looks like (e.g., 1st, 2:1, etc.; Distinction, Merit, etc.; or A, B, C, D, etc.). Setting out what the student is expected to do to be successful at each level of a tiered grading system helps them to make sense of the marking process while also facilitating self-management of their own expectations. Furthermore, it can also function as a useful resource for you if a student wants additional feedback about specific aspects of their performance once the marks have been released to them. As a reminder, an example of a truncated course catalog including the aims, objectives, learning outcomes, and other transferable skills is available to view in Chapter 6, Box 6.1.

Regarding assessment type, there are many methods you can use to assess your students and far too many for me to try and offer an exhaustive list here. It will depend on the discipline or practice you are teaching and what makes most sense for you and your students. You will also want to bear in mind the suitability of the assessment method in relation to the level and the character of the student cohort you are teaching.

Among the more commonly recognized methods of assessment are examinations (including oral, verbal, written, presentation), essays and reports, standardized tests (e.g., multiple-choice tests and other quizzes), project and portfolio work, and work-based learning. These are generic forms of assessment that can be tailored to your discipline or practice, the type of course, and the nature of the learning outcomes (i.e., whether the skills are academic or practical).

In Appendix 2 I have included a form you can use to demonstrate how each of your ILOs align with a topic or session number and how you intend each of them to be assessed or evaluated on your course. To get you started I have included some examples of each information point on the form. Following the principles of constructive alignment, after providing an initial statement of your course aims and objectives, list each ILO and, in association, clearly identify the topic or session number where these are covered, followed by a brief outline of how the ILO will be evaluated. This checklist will provide an audit trail for you to use as you plan your course, and may also be welcome as an audit trail to present to any other interested party, such as a program director, external examiner, or quality assessor.

Once you are satisfied with your aims, objectives, ILOs, and the forms of assessment and any feedback mechanisms, you are now ready to move on with the planning process for your course delivery.

7.6   DESIGNING A BLENDED-LEARNING TEACHING SESSION

Once the course aims, objectives, and learning outcomes have been established, you will be ready to start developing the specific content and methods of delivery. While it is likely that your course will be delivered using a linear structure, it may be that you plan to deliver specific topics organized within discrete teaching sessions or, where it is possible, to link similar subject content over several sessions (e.g., where there is a continuing theme). In this case it may make more sense to structure the delivery of your course around a series of separate units or modules. Alternatively, you may be planning to block-teach your course using a more intense mode of delivery over a much shorter timescale (e.g., several consecutive days).

However you structure the delivery, you will need to develop an outline of the intended content, including key concepts and theory, any practical activity, relevant resources that will be needed, and assessment and feedback points that will be incorporated into each of the teaching sessions or teaching units. Simultaneously, the course learning outcomes and other intended skills outcomes will be used to inform both the content and learning activities as well as how you decide to structure your course.

As you are already aware, aligning the learning outcomes with the course design is a key principle of the constructivist approach. You will find that this part of the planning process is iterative, where you will need to go back and forth between the design and the learning outcomes until you feel confident about the journey you will be taking your students on. It will also help you to map individual sessions with the course ILOs and other skills you intend to include, helping to give you clarity and confirm a purpose for each of your teaching sessions.

To help prepare students for learning, an outline plan of the content that students will encounter in each of the teaching sessions or teaching units should be developed. This should also include an indication of the time commitment to complete each unit, split between dependent and independent learning.[6] The next step is to develop a set of learning objectives that clearly identify the knowledge and/or skills that the student should expect to develop. This can be made available to students in the learning management system along with any other course material they will need in advance. For guidance, an example of a teaching unit outline is presented in Box 7.1.

BOX 7.1   EXAMPLE OF A UNIT OUTLINE

Welcome to Unit 1: Organizational Behavior: Individual-Level Behaviors

In this unit you will explore what organizational behavior is and what makes it effective from a range of different theoretical perspectives. You will analyze the different forms of individual behavior affected by a range of factors including motivation, personality, knowledge and learning, and communication. Finally, you will learn how attitudes impact the way an individual behaves at work.

Study time
This unit will take you approximately **16–20 hours** to complete. The unit includes 4 × 1-hour live workshops, and you will be expected to complete around 3–4 hours of preparatory work in advance of each live workshop. The preparatory element constitutes part of the independent learning on this module. Details of the preparation you will need to complete in advance of each workshop are available to you in the learning management system.

Unit objectives
Successful completion of this unit will help you to:

• define what organizational behavior is and differentiate it from other related concepts;
• define behavior in different contexts;
• define different types of motivation at work;
• examine personality from a nomothetic and idiographic perspective;
• examine behavioral and cognitive forms of learning in the workplace;
• examine communication and its relationship with perception.

When you have created the first unit or teaching session outline you will be ready to move on and design each of the remaining sessions. Of course, the design will depend on whether you prefer learning to be more tutor- or student-centered, but I am hoping that by now I have helped you to distinguish between a constructivist and instructivist learning style and recognize the additional benefits and opportunities that are presented by a move toward small-group delivery supported by a blended form of learning. As I have already mentioned, the traditional in-person lecture can still have a valuable part to play in teaching delivery in higher education, but I believe this needs to be used sparingly, and only when necessary, weaning students away from more passive forms of learning and toward more active forms of learning instead.

A model example of a flipped classroom, drawing on the design of a blended-learning approach, is displayed in Figure 7.1. Here, you can see the flipped design of the teaching session is dependent on a range of preparatory work that you set for your students. In line with the principles of a constructivist student-centered model of teaching, the tutor's role is to function as the session facilitator for the workshop activity. Using this design depends on your students joining the teaching session equipped with the knowledge they will need to be able to successfully work on an activity together, with the session tutor taking on more of a supportive role.

An example of a teaching session developed using a constructivist learning style and drawing from a blended form of learning using a flipped classroom approach is depicted in Table 7.1 and Table 7.2. In this example of a teaching plan, each learning session is completed in two parts. In Part 1, students are asked to prepare for the in-person teaching session (Part 2) by completing pre-session work using online materials that have been made available to them. Typically, they will have access to the online materials in a specific location, such as a school or faculty online learning management system where the course leader will have been able to upload the materials in advance, supported by an explanation of what the student is expected to do. The example shown in Table 7.1 presents a variety of tasks that could constitute the pre-learning for a synchronous teaching session. To successfully participate in Part 2 (the face-to-face teaching session presented in Table 7.2), the student will need to complete the pre-sessional work that has been set for them in Part 1. The pre-sessional work they have been set will typically include part of the independent learning and research that they are expected to complete during the course, and that has been identified in the course catalog.

That covers everything I want to say about the pre-delivery work. In Chapter 8 we can move on to the start of teaching and turn the spotlight onto the first phase of delivery and establish the guiding principles.

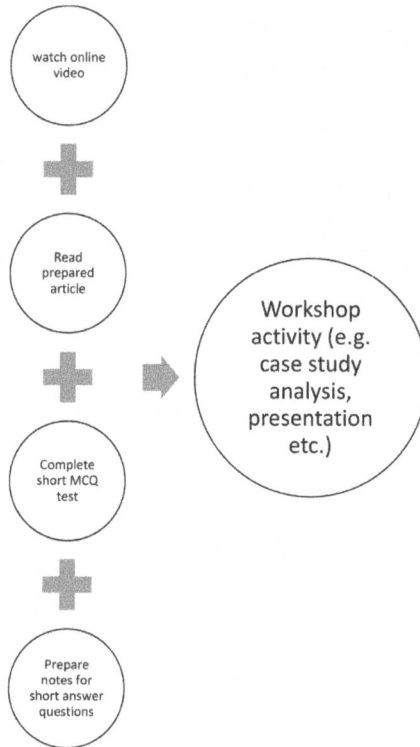

Figure 7.1   An example design of a flipped teaching session

7.7   CHAPTER SUMMARY

In this chapter I have presented the principles of a course design aimed at encouraging student-centered learning. I have set out the assumptions of constructive alignment as a triadic interactive framework, outlining the relationship between the course aims and objectives, the intended learning outcomes (ILOs), and how these inform course design. I emphasized the importance of recognizing the academic and practical skills your course will deliver and that these will influence how you shape the ILOs (i.e., whether the ILOs are weighted more toward the students developing intellectual or practical skills) and the teaching sessions, activities, and forms of assessment. The relationship between the format of delivery and various forms of assessment that you could consider aligning to your course was also discussed.

The final two sections of the chapter were dedicated to the role of pre-sessional work that your students need to complete before synchronous

Table 7.1   *Part 1: online (pre-workshop or pre-lecture) material*

Course code: xxxxxxx	
Topic Number: x (in a sequence of topics)	
Step number	Summary of step
1	Short video with module leader introducing what content will be covered in the online materials this week.
2	Text on screen introducing learning outcomes for the topic, and explicitly stating any links between the online materials and workshop activities.
3	Reading activity – students read pp. 220–225 and pp. 240–246 of the textbook.
4	Students to develop note-form answers on the following three questions: 1. What perspective does the author adopt? 2. What is the main argument of the author? 3. What global events in the past three years align with the author's perspective?
5	Students compare one short article with a second article and complete an MCQ test.
6	Theory of XXX – students watch a short video introducing this theory.

Table 7.2   *Part 2: face-to-face teaching*

Course code: xxxxxxx	
Topic Number: x (in a sequence of topics)	
Step number	Summary of step
1	Ask students to open polling application on their devices and join the poll.
2	Run in-class MCQ poll to check how well students have retained information from online material.
3	Review analytics from the MCQ poll, showing results on projector – highlight which areas students did not perform well on.
4	Spend 15 minutes recapping and exploring aspects of the online material where students have not performed as well. Explain which additional resources are available for students to deepen their understanding.
5	Activity – students log into the learning management system and access information that they will need to complete the workshop case study activity. Students work in small groups to develop solutions to the case study questions. Tutors work their way around the groups to discuss aspects of the case and potential solutions identified by the students.
6	Session finale and summary of outcomes. Each student group presents their case solution to the wider group, which leads into a more general tutor-facilitated workshop group discussion.

teaching delivery, an important element of the constructivist approach to teaching. The pre-sessional work forms part of the independent learning that the student will undertake on the module and encourages and enhances important constructivist values such as student autonomy, responsible learning, self-determination, and self-reflection, all of which are central to building an andragogical student-centered learning approach.

In Chapter 8 I will work through the various stages of course delivery in three distinct phases.

NOTES

1. Where this is the case, a course may be identified as 'foundation' (or 'beginners'), 'intermediate,' or 'advanced' level. It is more common in undergraduate studies where students may progress to the next level in the following year of the program once demonstrating that they have successfully achieved the learning outcomes at the current level they are studying.
2. Including shorter-duration video content that is more accessible than a weekly lecture typically delivered on a set day, at a set time, and in a set location.
3. Such as reading assignments and preparation work ahead of in-person teaching. The latter element usually forms part of the independent learning that is identified in the course catalog.
4. For example, either because you are not conversing in the student's first language or because challenging technical terms are being used.
5. For example, if it contributes to either formative or summative assessment, or where the group must present back their analysis to the wider group.
6. This usually includes the pre-work students are expected to complete for each teaching session.

8.   Course design: pulling it all together

8.1   INTRODUCTION

In this chapter I will bring together much of the discussion from Part I of the book and the first two chapters of Part II to help illustrate how you can develop your course and incorporate the approaches to learning presented to this point. I will do this in three phases that will capture the timeline of your delivery, starting with the planning and early delivery (Phase 1), and then moving to the intermediate stage where learning is in full flow and you may wish to introduce either a formative or summative assessment (Phase 2). The final stage (Phase 3) covers the period when the student will be working toward the completion of your course and may typically include a final summative assessment and an opportunity for students to reflect on their learning and how they will utilize this in their future learning.

8.2   PHASE 1 – PLANNING AND EARLY DELIVERY: BUILDING STUDENT CONFIDENCE, IDENTITY, AND INTERACTION

It is likely that you will be leading a diverse student cohort from a range of backgrounds and with varied experience. This will be your group of students and, in your role as course leader, they will look to you for direction, inspiration, and answers to a myriad of complex and challenging questions during the period when your course is active. Encouraging them to form both an identity and healthy interactions with you and their peers in this early transition period will lead to a better chance of them settling in and beginning to engage with the planned teaching sessions that you have so carefully designed.

There are several key factors that you will need to prioritize as you approach and enter Phase 1. While most, if not all, of these factors will remain relevant throughout your course, their relevance is even more prominent at the outset. In Appendix 3 I have set out a range of factors important to andragogical development as an inventory of objectives that you can target at your student group early in the course. To help you differentiate between factors I have categorized them in three sections. Section 1 and Section 2 objectives include a range of the attitudes and behaviors I discussed in Part I of the book, while

Section 3 objectives are pitched at skills development, referred to in Chapter 5 of Part I. This document can also function as a checklist when you feel you have completed the design stage. Once these factors have been established, some of them will be easy to maintain throughout and others you will need to continue working on to maintain.

Section 1 and Section 2 of the inventory are designed to get you thinking about what you can do to promote positive learning attitudes and behaviors among your students. Section 1 focuses on individual attributes and includes confidence, engagement, identity, and inclusivity. Section 2 relates to learning as a group and what you are going to do to promote positive group behaviors. Both sections are based on the content I discussed in Part I of the book, and it may be that you want to revisit these chapters to help you draw inspiration for your ideas. The most relevant chapter is indicated alongside each of the factors as they are presented. You should aim to address each objective and try to identify three actions for you to pursue and help support you in your efforts.

Section 3 is all about the development of skills and what you feel you can achieve during the delivery of your course. While you should aim to pursue all the objectives set out in sections 1 and 2 of the table, it will be more challeng-ing to address all the objectives set out in Section 3. For example, while you may be able to include possession skills as a learning objective, it may be more challenging to identify ways of helping students to develop both positioning and process skills. Even so, you should see this as more of a contribution to developing the students' skills, and any opportunity, no matter how small, could be a valuable experience for them and complement other opportunities they will encounter elsewhere. For example, perhaps you can invite a guest speaker from practice to talk at one of your live teaching sessions? This could open up other insightful opportunities for the students to communicate or join relevant networks through the guest speaker's own connections. Each opportunity is likely to be a unique experience for the students, so even this small contribution could result in a valuable career-related connection for one or more of your students.

Finally, and perhaps dependent upon your discipline and the type of skills that will be most valuable to your students, consider any other practical skills that could be included in your teaching and learning program that you believe may be conducive to their learning journey, both for the remainder of the program and after graduation.

I would strongly encourage you to have a go at completing as much of the form as you can. I have pointed you toward the relevant sections of the book where you can find more information associated with the objective in ques-tion. In addition to the discipline-related core content that you will teach your students, these objectives should be seen as the foundation stone of building a successful and worthwhile course that helps to extend the student experience.

8.2.1 Pre-Sessional Learning Activities

Throughout the text I have alluded to different methods of helping students to develop their positivity and encourage them to engage in your course. As I explained in Section 7.6 of Chapter 7, offering a range of pre-sessional learning activities can help you appeal to learners with different learning styles (e.g., visual, auditory, kinesthetic) while also supporting a better level of engagement for those students who are finding it difficult to focus on the content for long periods at a time. It also helps open up your course by being more inclusive of a range of learners. If pre-sessional learning is limited to reading a chapter of the textbook, or a long research paper, you will, for sure, lose some students who find it difficult to concentrate on long reading assignments. Some will switch off before they start, which will do nothing to enhance engagement.

Instead, try mixing up the pre-sessional learning activities. For example, offer them a short 5–10-minute video of either you or someone associated with your course explaining how a key theory or concept works, mixed with a short reading assignment, as then your students may feel more encouraged to give it a go. You can also point students toward the relevant chapter of the text for those who choose to engage in a more serious reading assignment, but if you offer some choice then there will be an increased likelihood that more students will have engaged to some extent with the class prep. If most students are in a position where they have covered enough learning to take the short test that you have also set them as part of the pre-sessional learning, then, once again, you are extending the hand of inclusivity by tempting more of your cohort to engage with at least some of the learning and feedback mechanisms that you have developed for your course.

Also, engaging with at least some of the pre-sessional learning should encourage more of your students to attend the synchronous teaching session because they have, at least in part, committed to the pre-learning. Encouraging student buy-in to the pre-sessional work should mean they are more motivated to extend that learning by joining you and their peers in the live teaching session.

And do not lose faith if some of your cohort does not engage with all aspects of the pre-sessional learning and the synchronous teaching. While this must be your aim, it is unrealistic for us to expect this. Some students will love your course and happily engage with all aspects, while others may not be so enthused. This latter group of students could still want to maximize their learning (or just want a good grade) and be diligent enough to engage in full, while the remainder may not be enthusiastic and may not be diligent students. You will need to work harder to engage these students, but you should stand a better chance if you offer a range of pre-sessional learning activities to encourage them to do so on their own terms.

8.3   PHASE 2 – INTERMEDIATE: DEVELOPING SKILLS, MID-TERM ASSESSMENT, AND FEEDBACK

Once the early sessions of your course are complete, you should be seeing visible signs that your students are settling in as they get used to the structure and patterns of delivery and start to form an identity. You will have started to pick out students who are keen or willing to regularly contribute to class debate. While it is valuable to know you can rely on the regular contributors to kick off class discussion and warm other students up in the process, I am also conscious at this stage of those students who feel less confident to air their views among the group and will aim to gently coax them into the discussions. Getting as many students as possible involved in class discussion will help to bring in a wider range of perspectives and this is more likely to stimulate other contributions, leading to better-informed and more representative debates.

8.3.1   Don't Panic!

While it is important to be vigilant and reflect on each teaching session, recognizing what went well and what did not work so well, it is all too easy to dwell on the negative outcomes. Even after many years of teaching there will be few able to profess that every session flows like a dream and their students leave the class with beaming faces. There is an adage that if we try to please everybody we just end up pleasing nobody. This can also be related to teaching.

Sessions that do not flow as well as we would like need to be kept in proportion, otherwise you could leave yourself vulnerable to making changes that are not necessary. I treat each teaching session as part of a broader learning curve, and while I am open to adapting what I do and how I do it, I am also conscious that the vibes I pick up from one group of students are not necessarily representative of how others will react. In fact, when you have multiple iterations of the same session to deliver, it is often tangible how one group of students will behave very differently to the next. Although it is often difficult to pinpoint why this is the case, there are some situational factors that may be out of your control and are accountable for student mood. For example, environmental factors, such as time of day, the aesthetics of the room, or students feeling anxious about an upcoming assessment, are all factors that can have an influence on how each of your cohorts will behave. Let us face it, the 9.00 am session is unlikely to be a good predictor of the 12.00 pm session, by which time students are likely to have more energy and so feel more creative.

Sessions timetabled for later in the day can also mean a drop in energy levels, which may mean you need to try and compensate for a subsequent drop in their motivation levels too.

8.3.1.1 ... but move the agenda forward

Let us take the perspective that the early part of your course delivery has gone to plan, and your students are, in the main, responding well and seem to be engaging. You are starting to gain their confidence and those early-stage barriers to interaction with both you and their peers are beginning to erode. Now is the time to try out new things. This might include purposefully mixing the student groups up while working together on an activity, or getting them up together at the front of class to present their findings rather than asking them to feedback from their desks. By the way, a word of caution about asking the students to present: if you intend to do this, I advise that, rather than putting each student on the spot at an early stage in the course, you let each group organize between them who will be the key presenters of feedback to the wider group.

By involving your students in these small activities, you will be starting to improve a range of skills, including elevated levels of interaction, group process and management skills, and presentation or public-speaking skills. Also, if your students are aware that there is an expectation on them to give feedback to the entire cohort, it will help focus them on the task, and to work on developing outcomes that are better designed and more meaningful. Importantly, when students share knowledge in this way and engage in the practice of peer learning with others who are likely to be at a similar stage, it can help to improve the process of understanding and sensemaking.

8.3.2 Mid-Term Assessment and Feedback

Whether your course is single or double semester, you should plan a formative assessment around the mid-point of the first period of delivery (i.e., the middle of Semester 1). If it is a single-semester course, then you will organize this to take place at the mid-point. If it is a two-semester course, then you should aim to introduce the formative assessment at the mid-point of each semester. Typically, two pieces of formative assessment are followed on each occasion by an end-of-semester summative assessment. You may arrange to organize this slightly differently, but the main point is that you include at least two opportunities per semester for students to complete some work and receive feedback on their progress. If your course is not delivered over the duration of a semester but is taught in a single block, the same principles will apply. You should aim to introduce a form of assessment halfway through the duration of the course to ensure the students are able to garner feedback on their learning progress.

The formative assessment you design may be standalone and will therefore have no direct correlation to the end-of-semester summative assessment. Ideally, you will aim to link the formative assessment to each piece of summative assessment, therefore enabling a stepped approach to learning. This will offer your students an opportunity to build their knowledge and skills by using the feedback from the formative assessment as feedforward to produce a better-informed piece of work for their summative assessment. This stepped approach should also help to allow a deeper form of learning to emerge from the course assessment.

However, let us not overlook the value that can also be achieved from standalone formative assessment or even by including two pieces of formative assessment, one standalone (short tests, MCQ assessment, etc.) and one linked to the summative assessment. Short formative assessments in the format of a test can easily be slotted in on a regular basis, being included either in the pre-learning component or during the in-person teaching session. If you are using an asynchronous form of delivery then it is possible you will be asking students to interpret and manage their own feedback, which can be made so much more meaningful if you are able to provide a written text to explore the correct (and incorrect) answer in more depth. There may be little benefit from a formative test if students are left to their own devices to understand why they did not select the correct answer.

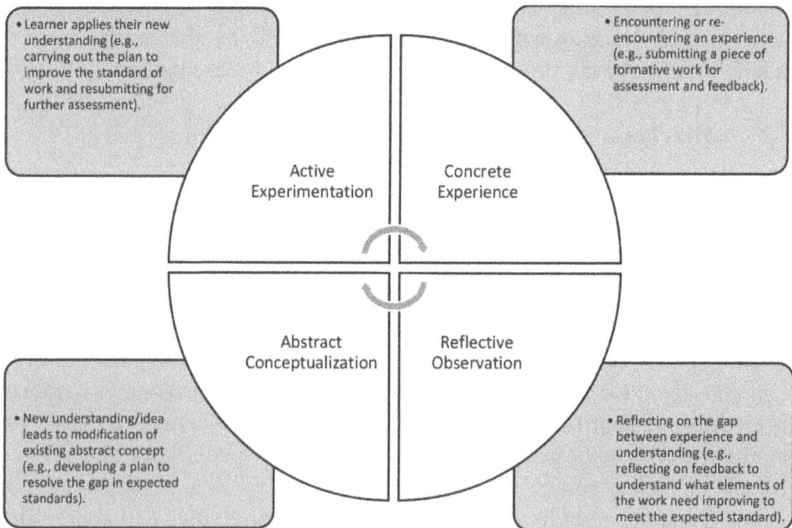

Source: Adapted from Kolb (2014).

Figure 8.1   *Experiential learning through assessment and feedback*

Drawing from David Kolb's (2014) Experiential Learning Cycle model to help illustrate how assessment and feedback supports learning development and future iterations of the same or similar submitted work, highlights how learning can be scaffolded[1] using linked formative and summative assessment. Figure 8.1 depicts the process through the lens of Kolb's model. In this illustration, submitting a piece of formative work for assessment and feedback would exemplify the concrete experience alluded to in Kolb's model. This could be a new experience for the learner or a reiteration of a previous experience, for example if the student is resubmitting their work or if the student has submitted a similar piece of work in the past. If the student is being assessed on a range of criteria, then it is possible that some of the criteria may be a new experience for them while they re-encounter other criteria being assessed. For example, if the student is submitting a formative essay for assessment, the subject of the essay may be a new experience for them, but they may re-encounter academic skills they have previously been assessed and received feedback on in some form (quality of their critical writing, referencing skills, etc.).

Once the student has received their feedback, they have an opportunity to reflect on where they have done well and where there needs to be further improvements in their work. This would equate to the Reflective Observation stage of the learning cycle and lead to the student developing a plan about what changes need to be made to bring their work up to a higher standard (the Abstract Conceptualization stage). Once the learner has understood from the feedback what is expected of them and devised a plan to improve their work (e.g., more critical analysis is needed), they will be ready to make those revisions (the Active Experimentation stage of Kolb's model) and resubmit for further assessment (returning to the Concrete Experience stage of the cycle). Typically, this stage would mean submission of the work for summative assessment (where formative and summative assessments are linked) or a further round of formative assessment.

Examining the relationship between formative and summative assessment where they have been linked helps to illustrate how, as Kolb intended, learning becomes a holistic process if managed in this way. According to Kolb, engaging with each stage, and therefore encountering the cycle in its entirety, is critical if learning is to be complete.

8.3.2.1 Feedback

Feedback comes in many different forms, from the behaviorist approach of reinforcement (e.g., delivered through short answer tests), through to critical review and analysis. Often referred to as a cognitivist approach, feedback that is given by critical review and analysis is typically offered to a passive receiver in the form of a directive that acts as a corrective function.

For comparison, Evans (2013) considers the socio-constructivist model of feedback where the tutor plays more of a facilitative role, offering the student feedback through comments and suggestions but then allowing the student autonomy to make their own revisions based on their personal insight and understanding. These new understandings can be enabled through dialogue with others, including both tutors and peers. In these situations, it is better to view feedback as an instrument to refine understanding of a concept or approach rather than as an all-encompassing corrective tool.

Whatever the format, feedback has been described by Hattie (1999) as the most powerful single moderator of improving student achievement. Feedback is recognized as an integral part of the learning experience (Cramp, 2011) and has been referred to as both 'feedforward' and 'feed up,' both in its role of supporting continued learning within the context of higher education and in its role in developing transferable skills that will pass with the student into future employment (Hounsell et al., 2008). Feedback should always be aimed at encouraging students to achieve their learning goals (i.e., improving the stand-ard and quality of their work) rather than at encouraging them to improve their performance goals (i.e., the mark they receive). Feedback can also be effective in other formats, so it may be better to use some of these alternative formats rather than always reverting to the use of written narrative. Let us consider a range of synchronous and asynchronous forms of feedback and the benefits that are offered by each.

Synchronous feedback, either in person or digitally communicated via a plat-form such as Zoom or Teams, can offer the benefits of real-time interaction that are not afforded by asynchronous delivery. Real-time interaction allows the student to check their understanding and make sense of their interpretation of your feedback. The level of interaction can be kept brief, particularly if you are under a tight deadline to complete the session, or you can plan for a more pro-tracted discussion that allows the student to raise penetrative questions about the subject matter. If you are delivering a face-to-face synchronous session to a large group (i.e., via lecture) then you could consider using a platform that students can access and join via their own electronic devices, allowing them a chance to raise questions digitally that can be displayed on-screen for other students attending the session to see. You can easily follow up by interacting with the entire group, responding verbally to each question in detail.[2]

If you are delivering the feedback session to your group online, then, once again, you can choose the format for the Q&A – for example, whether there is verbal interaction only or whether you will allow a mix of verbal and written questions (using a chat function, for example). I usually find giving students the option to ask questions either verbally or in written format encourages better participation. As mentioned above, you can also do this in person if students have access to a discussion board or similar platform while in the live in-person session. My preference is to encourage a verbal dialogue with students while in these settings, but offering this choice can be a method of bringing in those students who, perhaps due to experiencing social anxiety or where you are not communicating in their first language, are more reticent about speaking up in front of their peers. Offering this choice will therefore help to make these sessions more inclusive.

Using *asynchronous* formats for feeding back to students also has its benefits and can offer you a variety of different options. The format of asynchronous feedback should be guided by what you believe will be the most effective method for the students, but may also be dependent on your own preference (i.e., what is most straightforward for you to prepare). For example, as an alternative to providing written feedback you could consider using an audio-based message that will have the benefit of coming from a voice the students are familiar with. Going one step further, you could choose to develop video feedback, which may be particularly useful if you are explaining a diagram or, for example, demonstrating the impact of change to a model, or the outcomes from an experiment. Again, if the recording is delivered by the course leader or another well-known member of the teaching staff, familiarity with that person, and their trusted expertise, may make the recording more engaging for the student.

Finally, as an alternative method you could consider using peer feedback. This can be done most effectively in person within small groups, by asking students to exchange their work in class with their fellow group members, who will then familiarize themselves with the work and provide feedback to their peers based on their own observations. Or it can be managed within small groups asynchronously and online by encouraging each member to swap their work within the group for each group member to then provide feedback once they have familiarized themselves with the work. If the peer feedback method is used, it is important that it is facilitated by a member of the teaching team, who should be available in person, or via a recorded message if completed asynchronously. This is essential to address any questions and resolve any ambiguities that may occur during the feedback process.

Whatever the format and design of your feedback, there are some general guidelines that set a standard for what you should be aiming to achieve. Feedback should always aim to encourage the student to look toward the future and be seen as forming a part of the continuous learning loop. Therefore, feedback needs to:

- confirm the expected standard for the piece of assessment the students have been set;
- highlight existing good practice and help the students to understand what they have done well and why this is so;

- build on the above and include signposting so the student is clear about what needs to be improved and how they can go about doing this.

Valuable feedback helps the student to take control of their work going forward and so encourages the student-centered model of teaching you are striving to accomplish. As Archer (2010) highlights, good feedback supports the socio-constructivist viewpoint. Guided by tutor comments and suggestions, students can be encouraged to make the most of their autonomy and revise their work to enhance its quality. In groups and small learning communities, this leads to shared understanding where students will seek out and act on any feedback, emboldening them to take on responsibility for their work (Carless et al., 2011; Wenger et al., 2002). Once having had the chance to digest the feedback, the students should have some clarity about what they need to do to improve their work and the confidence to actively make those necessary improvements. In effect, they become active participants of the feedback process rather than mere receivers of feedback.

As highlighted in Kolb's (2014) model, reflection becomes a critical part of this feedback and learning process, and so it is important that you make abundantly clear to students any specific aspects of their returned work that warrant attention and where they need to reflect. To encourage reflection the tutor should aim to summarize the feedback that has been provided with key takeaways or learning points, highlighting where limitations or weaknesses of their work were most evident. Any such learning points should emphasize those things that would contribute most to improving the overall standard of their work. Examples of this could be to increase the number of sources used in the essay to help improve the quality of critical awareness, or allowing more time for planning and research at the outset of the assignment to help develop a more coherent structure. This will help the student connect with the bigger picture of what they need to improve to strengthen their academic work more generally, while more specific and nuanced feedback can be provided within the body of the work – for example, in a comments box within the margin.

Providing a long and detailed synopsis as a summary, one that includes many areas for improvement, may only dishearten the student and, in turn, discourage the growth mindset you are aiming to encourage. Don't forget, the principal aim of your feedback is to support the student so they can start closing any gaps that exist between where they are now and where they need to be to achieve the expected standards in their work.

From her extensive systematic review of 460 published articles on feedback in higher education, Evans (2013) identified a wide range of key principles for effective feedback practice, but went on to synthesize these into what she termed 12 pragmatic actions. I believe you will find these actions helpful to use as a checklist when you are designing assessment feedback mechanisms in your own course. These are the 12 pragmatic actions as proposed by Evans (2013, p. 79):

1. Ensuring an appropriate range and choice of assessment opportunities throughout a program of study.
2. Ensuring guidance about assessment is integrated into all teaching sessions.
3. Ensuring all resources are available to students via virtual learning environments and other sources from the start of a program to enable students to take responsibility for organizing their own learning.
4. Clarifying with students how all elements of assessment fit together and why they are relevant and valuable.
5. Providing explicit guidance to students on the requirements of assessment.
6. Clarifying with students the different forms and sources of feedback available, including e-learning opportunities.
7. Ensuring early opportunities for students to undertake assessment and obtain feedback.
8. Clarifying the role of the student in the feedback process as an active participant and not as purely a receiver of feedback and with sufficient knowledge to engage in feedback.
9. Providing opportunities for students to work with assessment criteria and to have access to work, with examples of good work.
10. Giving clear and focused feedback on how students can improve their work, including signposting the most important areas to address.
11. Ensuring support is in place to help students develop self-assessment skills, including training in peer feedback possibilities including peer support groups.
12. Ensuring training opportunities for staff to enhance shared understanding of assessment requirements.

While it may not be feasible for you to incorporate all 12 of Evans's actions into the design of your assessment feedback, I would aim to include as many as you believe feasible, dependent on the nature of the assessment tool you are intending to use (standard MCQ test(s), in-depth essay, lab-based experiment, group assignment, etc.) and the level of support you think students will need. Some of the actions may be more suitable to the nature of your assessment than others.

In addition to the actions set out by Evans, I would add that it is important to clearly state how the student should go about improving their performance where improvements have been identified as necessary. This could be accomplished, either unilaterally or in agreement with the student, by designing a formal plan of achievement goals that the student can work toward. You should also be mindful not to present feedback in a way that threatens the student's ego. Critique should always have a positive accent, reducing the risk of having negative connotations. This could be a particular problem for students who are low in self-efficacy.

8.4   PHASE 3 – THE END GAME: FINAL ASSESSMENT, REFLECTING ON LEARNING, AND INCORPORATING STUDENT LEARNING INTO NEXT STEPS

The end game comprises the closing stages of a long course that has been delivered throughout the entirety of an academic year. Or maybe it has been delivered using a block pattern of teaching and taken only a few days to complete. Alternatively, it is quite possible that the duration of the course falls somewhere in between these two extremes. Whatever the timeline, at this stage you will have delivered the bulk of the teaching and presented most, if not all, of the course content. So, hopefully, you will be well on target to meet those aims and objectives that you so carefully crafted before the outset of your course.

You will have successfully guided your students to a position where they will be ready to demonstrate their newfound knowledge and skills by successfully meeting the course learning outcomes. But this is not a time for letting up and feeling you are almost there. While you have successfully taken your students along the journey of learning and to a point in time where their hour is almost upon them, the most critical element of your course is about to begin as you enter the final phase: Phase 3.

The culmination of all your efforts – from the design and planning stage and the welcome and introduction you delivered to help your new students settle in, to the hours spent preparing for your teaching sessions, the ongoing feedback and evaluation of student progress, and, perhaps, the management of any pastoral care issues – is the final summative assessment. All roads lead to this, and how well you and your students oversee this final act will be a critical indicator of their success on your course.

There are still three important tasks that need to be fulfilled if students are to make the most of their learning:

1. You need to help your students prepare for their final summative assessment.
2. The students need to reflect on their learning from their time on your course.
3. You need to make sure they connect the learning from your course with learning on the wider program and with any future learning.

8.4.1 Helping Your Students Prepare

When it comes to the most suitable timing of your final piece of summative assessment, there are several possibilities depending on how many other pieces of summative assessment, if any, are used to assess your course. If your course is assessed by only a single piece of assessment it is highly likely that the submission of this piece will be scheduled close to the end point of teaching or, if an exam, the assessment will take place during the exam weeks, which are often positioned after the course teaching is complete. It is possible that you have more than one piece of summative assessment, in which case these will likely be scheduled at different points of time throughout the duration of your course. In this situation, it is usual that the final piece of summative assessment will make the biggest contribution to the overall course assessment. One of the benefits of this is that you can assure the students that all is still to play for and even if their progress has been slow or sporadic (or even non-existent) they can still turn things around and achieve a good grade.

While any responsibility for the students' preparation will be their own, just like a member of an orchestra who relies on the conductor for direction, they will look to you for guidance, support, and inspiration, and like the conductor you can play a key role in helping to bring the best out in them. You may decide to organize dedicated assessment support sessions, including using any final programed teaching as an interactive discussion seminar or a more formal lecture-style information dissemination session. You may also decide to include synchronous assessment preparation webinars with dedicated timeslots for different groups of students to attend.

It is also likely that students will want to contact you on a one-to-one basis for a more personal discussion about the assessment. However, unless you deem these to be necessary for a particular reason, such as to provide individualized feedback on formative assessment, or to discuss information that is either sensitive or unique to the student, I would advise against organizing dedicated one-to-one assessment support sessions. I tend to find most of the questions that are raised and discussed in these sessions are generic to the whole cohort and so the most efficient way of providing support and disseminating information is to make sure that other students are also present in those sessions, even if they merely join the session as interested observers and listen without raising any questions themselves. One of the problems that can arise with one-to-one support is inconsistent communication of information, often due to student misinterpretation. Small-group seminars, workshops, or lectures offer an environment that is much more conducive to consistent dissemination of information, and to avoiding misunderstandings.

I would also advise setting up a discussion board in your learning management system so that students can raise questions whenever they wish to do so.

Again, all students in the cohort should have access to the discussion board so that any questions raised by other students and addressed by you or other course tutors are visible for all to see. This will similarly increase consistency in communication and reduce student uncertainty through misunderstandings. It will also have the benefit of reducing, or even eliminating, one-to-one written communication from your students over email, a completely inefficient method of managing the same information that may be pertinent to many in your group.

If you do make use of a discussion board or similar, make sure that you respond to any questions on a regular basis if you want to encourage students to use this as the principal method of communicating with you. You can also recommend that students read the discussion board in its entirety to pick up lots of useful assessment-related information. If you manage the system yourself, you will have the benefit of knowing that students are receiving accurate and prompt information. When there is a communication void, and the students are unable to get a response from either you or someone else from the course teaching team, it is quite possible that, in their uncertainty, they will turn to each other to seek answers, which is often when misnomers and misinformation will arise.

8.4.2   Reflect on Learning

The opportunity to reflect may be embedded in a variety of ways. You could ask students to provide a reflective piece in their final summative assessment, either as a separate and standalone piece of assessment or integrated as a section of the main assessment. Alternatively, prior to introducing the final piece of summative assessment, you could introduce a piece of formative assessment where students are asked to reflect on their time on your course. The benefit of this may be reciprocal because, while the student will receive some feedback on the quality of their reflective statement/essay, you can benefit from qualitative feedback on their experience, which may be used to identify any potential refinements you could make before the next delivery of your course.

Some programs include a separate course that will ask students to integrate their learning experience on the wider program and capture this in a reflective essay, either as formative or as summative assessment. My own course is delivered to students from a range of programs in the Business School, and each of these programs includes a professional development course that forms a compulsory element of the students' Level 1 journey. As part of the assessment on these professional development courses, students are asked to write a reflective account of their learning across the wider program.

You could also ask students to keep a reflective log or diary that captures key outcomes or events from their time on your course. Extracts from the logs can then be used to form an element of the final formative or summative assessment. The ability to reflect on their learning is an important skill that will help students identify their strengths and weaknesses, enabling them to strategize their learning going forward.

8.4.3   Connecting Their Learning

Finally, students need to connect their learning from your course with past, current, and future learning on the wider program.

Your constructively aligned course ensures your students are formally assessed on the learning outcomes, and so how well they measure up to these will be key to the students' success. Explaining the relationship between the course learning outcomes and assessment will help students to make sense of what you are asking them to do. But also, addressing how your course outcomes are informed by the wider program learning outcomes will add an additional level of granularity to this process. Joining up all three aspects – program learning outcomes, course learning outcomes, and the assessment they are about to undertake – will help the student make sense of the outcomes from their learning, the way they are being assessed, and how all of this relates to the wider program.

I have tried to capture these essential relationships in Figure 8.2.

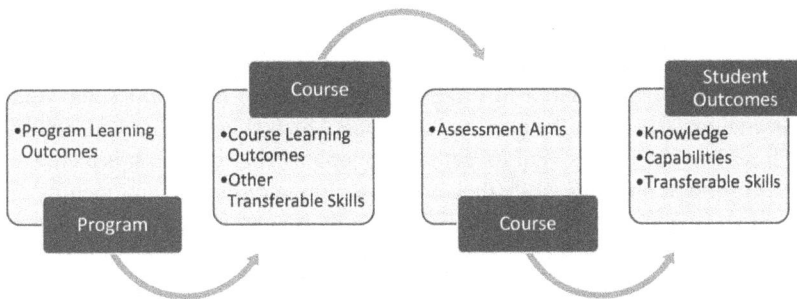

Figure 8.2   Alignment of program and course learning outcomes with the aims of the assessment

Here, once again, you can see how each phase aligns as the program learning outcomes inform the development of the course learning outcomes and other transferable skills, which, in turn, inform the course assessment aims. This should lead to the student leaving at the end of your course enlightened through learning new knowledge and skills that they can transfer to other situations and experiences, whether this is on other courses they will need to complete or after they have graduated.

If you plan to deliver an assessment preparation lecture or small teaching group session, then I would encourage you to include an overview in that session of the connections between the program aims, course aims, and the way the course is assessed. Taking time out to make these connections clear will help the students see the purpose of the learning they have completed and illustrate how they will be able to put their learning to effective use going forward. Helping students to understand the connection between the program aims, course aims, and the way they will be assessed could form part of any reflective work undertaken by the students at the end of the course that I have referred to in the previous section.

8.5   CHAPTER SUMMARY

The purpose of this chapter has been to consider the practicalities of course design, drawing on the student perspective as set out in Part I of the text and the practical and theoretical arguments that help to set out a strategy in chapters 6 and 7. I have included suggestions about the overall design of teaching, the learning activities, how you will assess and provide feedback, and how you will ensure to capture all of this within a constructively aligned framework, guided by the program and course intended learning outcomes. Amid all this, the main consideration is the student and how their needs become the central thread that guides any course design. In Chapter 8 I have presented this case within a logical sequence of three phases, connecting into the all-important pre-phase work I discussed in Chapter 7 that sets the foundations for your course and will become the guiding light upon which everything else depends.

Phase 1 of delivery is vital for setting the tone of your course. It is a crucial time to support students while they are developing confidence and identity at the start, helping them to feel more secure in their communications and inter- actions. Phase 2 covers the mid-session delivery of your course and includes the important aspect of assessment in both its formative and summative guises. At this stage, summative assessment is more likely to be pertinent to a long course, but whatever the case it is clear how critical good forms of formative assessment are for the student and their ability to grow in confidence and make sense of the material covered in your course. Finally, the end phase (Phase 3) is a time for encouraging students to reflect and consolidate their learning before the all-important final summative assessment is upon them. This is also a time for encouraging your students to think about the process of continuity and how they will take their learning forward along with the skills they have developed on your course, enabling them to make effective use of this learning and these skills in the future.

NOTES

1. Scaffolding is an important element of the constructivist approach to learning and refers to the process of providing initial support to assist the learner with the objective of gradually removing support as the learner begins to develop confidence with the task or learning activity/event. The aim is to encourage the learner to become independent of any need for instructional support as they transcend into becoming a more independent learner.

2. If you offer students a choice to raise questions either verbally or digitally you will get a much better participation rate, particularly in a large group. However, I would recommend encouraging a verbal response to each question raised where possible. If the session is recorded, students who were unable to attend can also benefit from the Q&A and it can also be revisited by students later. This will help to make the most efficient use of your time, because it could save you needing to correspond individually with students later.

9.   Conclusion

9.1   SCOPE

My principal aim while authoring this book has been to help support academics in their role as course leaders by offering a context for course design that includes many of the key issues experienced by higher education students. While I feel the content may be most helpful for those of you who are starting out on your academic and teaching careers, hopefully I can also inspire the more seasoned academic with some fresh ideas as they approach their new designs or course restructures. The content of this book should also appeal to program directors who are tasked with delivering a program that is attractive to students and based on andragogic outcomes that the latter will find of practical use to help them meet the skills agenda in the contemporary workplace.

So, I set out the case that, with regard to enhancing practice, the book's main audience will be course leaders and program directors, both of whom have a personal stake in course design, though the broad thesis of this text and its wider connotations may also be of interest to a more extensive audience in higher education, including directors of student education as they reconsider their existing offer to students and how this aligns with current and future changes within the sector.

I am also conscious that some of the fundamental issues and remedial actions set out in the text will resonate with other post-compulsory educators. For example, anyone teaching or working in further education technical colleges and involved in the design of courses and programs will find there is broad overlap in the aims of both Part I and Part II of the book with what they aim to achieve within their own andragogic or pedagogic sphere of activity.

9.2   A NEW LENS ON THE FAMILIAR

In reaching this point you should now be conversant with the key arguments that I have presented. I have maintained the central thread throughout that by having a better understanding of our students we can respond more effectively to their needs by positioning our teaching to better meet them and, as a consequence, enhance their student experience while studying on our programs. In doing so, I have presented a core thesis that student-centered learning is the most effective way of helping the student to grow in confidence and cultivate a positive mindset. This is best achieved through us adopting a constructivist paradigm of learning, drawing on the principles of developing active rather than passive learners.

I have set out a plan in Part I of the book for helping to mitigate some of the students' key challenges. In Part II I have distinguished between a constructivist and instructivist approach to teaching methodology, while arguing the case for a course design informed by the principles of constructive alignment. As part of the toolkit for course design, I have also included a range of practical suggestions and tips that are incorporated into a three-stage process for design and are aimed at supporting a constructivist paradigm of teaching.

In addition to the existing research that I have utilized to help justify and inform my approach, in writing this book I have drawn from my own experiences of teaching, both from the pre-pandemic and from the post-pandemic world. My reference to 'post-pandemic' as though it raises the prospect of some kind of dividing line between two different epochs of learning mainly comes down to the digital enhancement of our teaching methods and materials that has encouraged us to transform the way we deliver learning to students – a period of change during what became known as the 'pandemic years.'[1] While I am sure we all agree that there were many challenges during this time and that the learning curve was often steep, it helped us to become more learned and speed up our inevitable transition to more digitally informed ways of teaching delivery. I know for certain that I found this to be the case, and I have tried to bring in some of my own experiences from the transition as well as those things that, as we lose some of our skepticism and more readily embrace digital forms of learning, continue to work well for me post-transition.

9.2.1 Reflection

When I reflect on my time since starting out as a course leader, I reminisce on the changes I have made to the style of teaching I adopted then and how I now approach both my style of teaching and the strategies I use for designing a course. Some of these changes have been subtle, arising through trial and error (i.e., learning what works better), but some have been more radical, mainly in response to the change in the teaching climate that has occurred over recent years. In part, these changes have also been driven by a shift in the expectations of students who enter higher education, which, in turn, have been driven by societal changes, including a market model for higher education and the broad range of skills now demanded of graduates by many employers.

As I look back, I can remember that in those days I had a much more tutor-centered approach to teaching, which gave me more control over the narrative in situations of large- or even small-group learning. I organized the structure and format of those early sessions around a series of core messages that were largely disseminated to a passive audience. While taking this 'safety-first' approach means there is less opportunity for your audience to ask questions that you may find challenging and difficult to address with accuracy in front of a group of students, it is an approach that is far less supportive of their learning.

As my confidence grew over the first few months in post, my priorities soon began to change, with a shift in my focus to a much more interactive style of teaching that gave my students voice and enabled them to take part in livelier and learned debates. This meant that my focus shifted from shielding myself with a 'safety-first' approach to tackling the real task at hand, that is, using the most effective methods of supporting student learning. A student-centered approach allows students to develop their own personalities in class.

As you become a more confident tutor you will begin to see your students as individuals rather than just a homogeneous group. Even though it is still probable with large class sizes that you will not have the time to get to know your students individually, knowing the potential challenges they face will broaden your understanding of their behavior. While this should help you to prepare before you meet them in your first teaching session, understanding your students, their capabilities, their expectations, and the challenges they face provides material information that you will also find helpful as you begin the pre-phase work on your course design.

Hopefully, in authoring this book I have been able to support you in some way along your journey of course design. As we set out to do what is best for our students it helps to understand what this means and how we intend to get there. After working your way through Part I and Part II of the book you will hopefully feel better equipped to answer these questions and begin developing an outline plan for your course, starting with the intended learning outcomes that will help to inform the mode of delivery and methods of assessment.

But during your own time for reflection, it is imperative that you take time out to recognize the positive impact you will have had in other ways, helping students grow in confidence and maturity and contributing toward the life-long learning skills that will be so critical to them throughout their journey, wherever that takes them. These are often the achievements that we, in our role as academics, fail to recognize with our busy schedules as we move on to the next project or task. Promise yourself that you will take time out as part of your teaching reflection to include these important aspects of your role and your contribution to student growth.

9.3   AND FINALLY …

In writing this book I set out by highlighting in Chapter 1 some of the more generic challenges that confront students when they begin their journey in higher education. These challenges include coming to terms with a new concept of being an 'independent' learner while also grappling with their own expectations of becoming a university student. As we know, when expectations collide with reality the experience can be difficult to embrace.

This leads me to a point I briefly alluded to in Chapter 1, that attrition rates are a principal concern, particularly for undergraduates starting out on a new life that leaves behind the sense of security offered by the close confines of secondary education. Attrition in some programs can be a significant issue that becomes one of the key indicators of the program's success or failure. In the business model adopted by many universities, this may mean a lingering threat of program closure as financial pressures take center stage.

So, from an institutional perspective there seem to be many reasons why student welfare and engagement will take priority, not least, of course, because universities have a duty of care to their charges. Returning once again to the higher education funding model, we find it is increasingly the case that programs today need to be financially viable to justify their existence. Programs that are not attracting enough students through enrolment may offer clear-cut cases for further scrutiny and potential removal from the school's or faculty's portfolio. However, where there is plenty of initial interest but high attrition rates, this will, quite naturally, raise questions too, including questions about the quality of program delivery. While within the ambitions of this book it is beyond my remit to investigate the plethora of reasons why this could be the case, the point about developing a course to meet contemporary higher education student needs is central to the thrust of this argument.

Whatever your role in education, I wish you every success in the future.

NOTE

1. A period roughly stretching from February 2020 to the end of 2022 depending on where you were located at the time. For many this meant communicating in a virtual environment using digital technology and very little (if any) in-person teaching (once again, depending on where you were located at the time).

Appendix 1: marking criteria for group written report (example of detailed marking criteria for summative assessment)

Table A1.1   *Marking criteria for group written report*

Criterion	Grade				
	Fail	III	II.2	II.1	First
Structure & Organization: statement of aims, logical order of material, focus on question, conclusion	Disorganized. No structure, aims or conclusion.	Some attempt at structure or organization but inappropriate.	Structure attempted. Evidence of organization. Sound aims and conclusion.	Mostly well organized. Appropriate structure. Aims and a conclusion specified.	Well organized throughout. Good structure. Appropriate aims and a clearly specified conclusion.
Coverage: comprehensiveness, evidence of research, reading; use of data sources	Lack of coverage. Little or no use made of source material or literature. May draw narrowly on lecture material rather than showing evidence of research.	Lack of breadth in use of relevant source material or literature, although some attempt made to research answer. Problems with selection of data or other empirical evidence.	Fairly comprehensive use of material but some notable omissions. Some problems with use of data or other empirical evidence.	Fairly comprehensive coverage of material. Good use of data sources or other empirical evidence.	A thorough understanding of the relevant source material and literature. Comprehensive coverage of material. Excellent use of data sources and empirical evidence.

Criterion	Grade				
	Fail	III	II.2	II.1	First
Critical ability	Critique of literature or data sources often absent. If present, demonstrates an inability to distinguish high-quality from poor-quality literature or data.	Critique of literature or data shows some ability to separate significant and relevant from trivial and irrelevant, but little ability to evaluate the quality of the data or literature; takes literature at face value.	Critique of literature or data shows some ability to separate significant and relevant from trivial and irrelevant, some ability to discern the significance of data, and some ability to evaluate the quality of the data or literature, but often takes literature at face value.	Critique of literature or data shows an ability to separate significant and relevant from trivial and irrelevant, an ability to discern the significance of data, and some ability to evaluate the quality of the data or literature.	Critique of literature and data shows an unfailing ability to separate significant and relevant from the trivial and irrelevant, an ability to discern the significance of data, and perceptive and well-reasoned evaluations of data or literature.
Accuracy and understanding of material	Fails to address the question posed. Fails to demonstrate understanding of the subject.	Inaccuracies evident. Some limited understanding of the subject, not applied to the question.	Sound understanding of the subject but not effectively focused on the question. Some inaccuracies or misunderstand-ings.	Good understanding of the subject, most focused on the question.	Accurate and thorough understanding focused on the question throughout.

	Grade				
Criterion	Fail	III	II.2	II.1	First
Presentation: legibility, grammar, spelling, clarity of expression	Use of English so poor as to obscure the sense of what is written. Tables, figures, etc. unclear and undefined.	Largely correct in spelling and grammar. Use of English so poor as to obscure the sense of what is written in a few places. Tables, figures, etc. usually clearly set out: all items defined by title, column, or row headings or notes.	Largely correct in spelling and grammar. Use of English hardly ever so poor as to obscure the sense of what is written. Tables, figures, etc. usually clearly set out: all items defined by title, column, or row headings or notes.	Correct in spelling and grammar. Use of English never so poor as to obscure the sense of what is written. Tables, figures, etc. clearly set out: all items defined by title, column, or row headings or notes.	Of the same standard as a published article. Correct in spelling and grammar. Fluent use of English: a delight to read. Tables, figures, etc. clearly set out: all items defined by title, column, or row headings or notes.
Presentation: citations & references	No consistent referencing system. References not cited; citations not referenced. References give too few details to enable the location of the reference. No refs = No marks.	Uses an inconsistent referencing system and some details may be missing. Some sources cited fail to appear in the List of References; some items in the List of References not cited in the essay.	Uses an inconsistent referencing system but no details missing. Some sources cited fail to appear in the List of References; some items in the List of References not cited in the essay.	Uses the Harvard referencing system. All sources cited appear in the List of References; no items in the List of References not cited in the essay.	Uses the Harvard referencing system. All sources cited appear in the List of references; no items in the List of References not cited in the essay.

Appendix 2: course alignment

Figure A2.1   Course alignment

Table A2.1   Course alignment

Course aims/objectives:		
Intended learning outcome (ILO)	Topic/session number where ILO is included in the content	How will the ILO be evaluated?
1. By the end of this course students will be able to critically analyze competing theoretical perspectives of …	2 & 9	Semester 1* and Semester 2** summative assessments
2. By the end of this course students will be able to identify and describe the relationship between … and …	5 & 11	Semester 1* summative assessment
3. By the end of this course students will be able to demonstrate their understanding of … (including … and …) and its impact on the environment	1, 2, 5, 7, & 10	Semester 1* summative assessment
4. By the end of this course students will have achieved a level of proficiency in … and improved their … skills to help develop solutions to practical problems arising in the discipline	3, 5, 6, 8, 9, & 11	Semester 1* summative assessment

Course aims/objectives:		
Intended learning outcome (ILO)	Topic/session number where ILO is included in the content	How will the ILO be evaluated?
5. By the end of this course students will be able to apply critical-thinking skills to the subject discipline of ...	2	Semester 1* and Semester 2** summative assessment

Notes:
* Semester 1 Assignment: For the first piece of summative assessment, students will be asked to critically appraise and answer a range of questions relating to a case study scenario that they will be presented with midway through Semester 1.
** Semester 2 Exam: For the second piece of summative assessment, students will be asked to complete a two-hour exam during the summer exam period.

Appendix 3: inventory of objectives

Table A3.1   Inventory of objectives

Section 1: Individual Differences – How will I develop student:		
Objective	Location	Actions per objective
Confidence?	Chapter 3	1.
		2.
		3.
Engagement?	Chapter 4	1.
		2.
		3.
Identity?	Chapter 4	1.
		2.
		3.
Inclusivity?	Chapter 3 & Chapter 4	1.
		2.
		3.
Section 2: Group Behavior – How will I:		
Build a trusting rapport with my students?	Chapter 4	1.
		2.
		3.
Develop community within the group?	Chapter 4	1.
		2.
		3.
Encourage interaction between my students?	Chapter 4	1.
		2.
		3.
Promote a growth mindset among my students?	Chapter 3	1.
		2.
		3.

Section 3: Skills Development – Will there be opportunities for students to develop:		
Possession skills (interpersonal skills, communication skills, etc.)?	Chapter 5	
Positioning skills (developing social connections and networks in relation to future careers)?		
Process skills (career self-management skills, e.g., understanding the labor market; developing good interview/assessment center skills, etc.)?		
Other practical skills I would like to focus on:		How will you embed these skills into your course?

References

Archer, J.C. (2010). State of the science in health professional education: Effective feedback. *Medical Education, 44*(1), 101–108. https://doi.org/10.1111/j.1365-2923.2009.03546.x.

Aylward, R.C., & Cronje, J.C. (2022). Paradigms extended: How to integrate behaviorism, constructivism, knowledge domain, and learner mastery into instructional design. *Educational Technology Research and Development, 70*(2), 503–529.

Azevedo, A., Apfelthaler, G., & Hurst, D. (2012). Competency development in business graduates: An industry-driven approach for examining the alignment of undergraduate business education with industry requirements. *The International Journal of Management Education, 10*(1), 12–28. https://doi.org/10.1016/j.ijme.2012.02.002.

Baeten, M., Kyndt, E., Struyven, K., & Dochy, F. (2010). Using student-centred learning environments to stimulate deep approaches to learning: Factors encouraging or discouraging their effectiveness. *Educational Research Review, 5*(3), 243–260. https://doi.org/10.1016/j.edurev.2010.06.001.

Ballantine, J., Guo, X., & Larres, P.M. (2018). Can future managers and business executives be influenced to behave more ethically in the workplace? The impact of approaches to learning on business students' cheating behavior. *Journal of Business Ethics, 149*(1), 245–258. https://doi.org/10.1007/s10551-016-3039-4.

Balloo, K., Pauli, R., & Worrell, M. (2017). Undergraduates' personal circumstances, expectations and reasons for attending university. *Studies in Higher Education, 42*(8), 1373–1384. https://doi.org/10.1080/03075079.2015.1099623.

Bandura, A. (1997). *Self-Efficacy: The Exercise of Control*. New York: W.H. Freeman and Company.

Beatson, N., Berg, D., & Smith, J.K. (2019). The Sheldon effect: Fixed mindset does not always mean fragile confidence. *Accounting Education, 28*(5), 532–552. https://doi.org/10.1080/09639284.2019.1661858.

Biggs, J. (1996). Enhancing teaching through constructive alignment. *Higher Education, 32*(3), 347–364. https://doi.org/10.1007/bf00138871.

Biggs, J. (2003). *Aligning Teaching and Assessing to Course Objectives. Teaching and Learning in Higher Education: New Trends and Innovations*. University of Aveiro. [Online] Accessed 21 August 2023. Available from: Aligning_teaching_and_assessing_to_course_objectiv.pdf.

Biocca, F., Harms, C., & Burgoon, J.K. (2003). Toward a more robust theory and measure of social presence: Review and suggested criteria. *Presence: Teleoperators and Virtual Environments, 12*(5), 456–480. https://doi.org/10.1162/105474603322761270.

Black, P., & Wiliam, D. (1998). Inside the black box: Raising standards through classroom assessment. *Phi Delta Kappan, 80*(2), 139–148. http://www.jstor.org/stable/20439383.

Boud, D., Dawson, P., Bearman, M., Bennett, S., Joughin, G., & Molloy, E. (2018). Reframing assessment research: Through a practice perspective. *Studies in Higher Education, 43*(7), 1107–1118. https://doi.org/10.1080/03075079.2016.1202913.

Brzeski, A. (2017). Literacy practices, identity and engagement: Integrating multifaceted identities of college students to support learning. *Research in Post-Compulsory Education, 22*(3), 391–408. https://doi.org/10.1080/13596748.2017.1358519.

Burger, E. (2012). Teaching to fail. *Inside Higher Education*, 20 August, p. 21.

Byrne, M., Flood, B., & Willis, P. (2002). The relationship between learning approaches and learning outcomes: A study of Irish accounting students. *Accounting Education, 11*(1), 27–42. https://doi.org/10.1080/09639280210153254.

Cain, A., Grundy, J., & Woodward, C.J. (2018). Focusing on learning through constructive alignment with task-oriented portfolio assessment. *European Journal of Engineering Education, 43*(4), 569–584. https://doi.org/10.1080/03043797.2017.1299693.

Carless, D., Salter, D., Yang, M., & Lam, J. (2011). Developing sustainable feedback practices. *Studies in Higher Education, 36*(4), 395–407. https://doi.org/10.1080/03075071003642449.

Carroll, J.M., & Iles, J. (2006). An assessment of anxiety levels in dyslexic students in higher education. *British Journal of Educational Psychology, 76*(3), 651–662. https://doi.org/10.1348/000709905x66233.

CBI & Pearson Education. (2016). *Education and Skills Survey: The Right Combination.* [Online] Accessed 16 August 2023. Available from: https://epale.ec.europa.eu/sites/default/files/cbi-education-and-skills-survey2016.pdf.

Choi, B. (2021). I'm afraid of not succeeding in learning: Introducing an instrument to measure higher education students' fear of failure in learning. *Studies in Higher Education, 46*(11), 2107–2121. https://doi.org/10.1080/03075079.2020.1712691.

Cohen, E.G. (1994). Restructuring the classroom: Conditions for productive small groups. *Review of Educational Research, 64*(1), 1–35. https://doi.org/10.3102/00346543064001001.

Cohen, L., Manion, L., & Morrison, K. (2017). *Research Methods in Education.* London: Routledge.

Cole, M.T., Shelley, D.J., & Swartz, L.B. (2014). Online instruction, e-learning, and student satisfaction: A three year study. *The International Review of Research in Open and Distributed Learning, 15*(6). https://doi.org/10.19173/irrodl.v15i6.1748.

Cook, A., & Leckey, J. (1999). Do expectations meet reality? A survey of changes in first-year student opinion. *Journal of Further and Higher Education, 23*(2), 157–171. https://doi.org/10.1080/0309877990230201.

Cox, A.M., Daoud, M., & Rudd, S. (2013). Information Management graduates' accounts of their employability: A case study from the University of Sheffield. *Education for Information, 30*(1–2), 41–61. https://doi.org/10.3233/efi-130929.

Cramp, A. (2011). Developing first-year engagement with written feedback. *Active Learning in Higher Education, 12*(2), 113–124. https://doi.org/10.1177/1469787411402484.

DeWitt, J., & Archer, L. (2015). Who aspires to a science career? A comparison of survey responses from primary and secondary school students. *International Journal of Science Education, 37*(13), 2170–2192. https://doi.org/10.1080/09500693.2015.1071899.

Diseth, Å. (2003). Personality and approaches to learning as predictors of academic achievement. *European Journal of Personality, 17*(2), 143–155. https://doi.org/10.1002/per.469.

Diseth, Å. (2007). Students' evaluation of teaching, approaches to learning, and academic achievement. *Scandinavian Journal of Educational Research, 51*(2), 185–204. https://doi.org/10.1080/00313830701191654.

Dobransky, N.D., & Frymier, A.B. (2004). Developing teacher–student relationships through out of class communication. *Communication Quarterly*, *52*(3), 211–223. https://doi.org/10.1080/01463370409370193.

Donald, W.E., Baruch, Y., & Ashleigh, M. (2017). The undergraduate self-perception of employability: Human capital, careers advice, and career ownership. *Studies in Higher Education*, *44*(4), 599–614. https:// doi .org/ 10 .1080/ 03075079 .2017 .1387107.

Dweck, C.S. (2014). *Self-Theories: Their Role in Motivation, Personality, and Development.* New York: Psychology Press. https://doi.org/10.4324/9781315783048.

Dweck, C. (2017). *Mindset: Changing the Way You think to Fulfil Your Potential.* Updated Edition. London: Robinson.

Entwistle, N.J., Hanley, M., & Hounsell, D. (1979). Identifying distinctive approaches to studying. *Higher Education*, *8*(4), 365–380. https://doi.org/10.1007/bf01680525.

Evans, C. (2013). Making sense of assessment feedback in higher education. *Review of Educational Research*, *83*(1), 70–120. https://doi.org/10.3102/0034654312474350.

Faranda, W.T. (2015). The effects of instructor service performance, immediacy, and trust on student–faculty out-of-class communication. *Marketing Education Review*, *25*(2), 83–97. https://doi.org/10.1080/10528008.2015.1029853.

Faranda, W.T., Clarke, T.B., & Clarke, I. (2021). Marketing student perceptions of academic program quality and relationships to surface, deep, and strategic learning approaches. *Journal of Marketing Education*, *43*(1), 9–24. https://doi.org/10.1177/0273475320939261.

Feigenbaum, P. (2021). Telling students it's O.K. to fail, but showing them it isn't: Dissonant paradigms of failure in higher education. *Teaching and Learning Inquiry*, *9*(1), 13–27. http://dx.doi.org/10.20343/teachlearninqu.9.1.4.

Fraser, C.J., Duignan, G., Stewart, D., & Rodrigues, A. (2019). Overt and covert: Successful strategies for building employability skills of vocational education graduates. *Journal of Teaching and Learning for Graduate Employability*, *10*(1), 157–172. https://doi.org/10.21153/jtlge2019vol10no1art782.

Fuller, A., Heath, S., & Johnston, B. (eds) (2011). *Rethinking Widening Participation in Higher Education: The Role of Social Networks.* London: Routledge. https://doi .org/10.4324/9780203817056.

Furrer, C., & Skinner, E.A. (2003). Sense of relatedness as a factor in children's academic engagement and performance. *Journal of Educational Psychology*, *95*(1), 148–162. https://doi.org/10.1037/0022-0663.95.1.148.

Gillock, K.L., & Reyes, O. (1999). Stress, supports, and academic performance of urban, low-income, Mexican-American adolescents. *Journal of Youth and Adolescence*, *28*(2), 259–282. https://doi.org/10.1023/A:1021657516275.

Gray, F.E. (2010). Specific oral communication skills desired in new accountancy graduates. *Business and Professional Communication Quarterly*, *73*(1), 40–67. https:// doi.org/10.1177/1080569909356350.

Hailkari, T., Virtanen, V., Vesalainen, M., & Postareff, L. (2022). Student perspectives on how different elements of constructive alignment support active learning. *Active Learning in Higher Education*, *23*(3), 217–231. https:// doi .org/ 10 .1177/ 1469787421989160.

Harvey, A., & Kamvounias, P. (2008). Bridging the implementation gap: A teacher-as-learner approach to teaching and learning policy. *Higher Education Research and Development*, *27*(1), 31–41. https://doi.org/10.1080/07294360701658716.

Hattie, J. (1999). *Influences on Student Learning.* Inaugural lecture, University of Auckland, 2 August.

Hillman, D.C.A., Willis, D.J., & Gunawardena, C.N. (1994). Learner–interface interaction in distance education: An extension of contemporary models and strategies for practitioners. *American Journal of Distance Education, 8*(2), 30–42. https://doi.org/10.1080/08923649409526853.

Holmes, L. (2013). Competing perspectives on graduate employability: Possession, position or process? *Studies in Higher Education, 38*(4), 538–554. https://doi.org/10.1080/03075079.2011.587140.

Horwitz, F.M. (2013). An analysis of skills development in a transitional economy: The case of the South African labour market. *The International Journal of Human Resource Management, 24*(12), 2435–2451. https://doi.org/10.1080/09585192.2013.781438.

Hounsell, D., McCune, V., Hounsell, J., & Litjens, J. (2008). The quality of guidance and feedback to students. *Higher Education Research and Development, 27*(1), 55–67. https://doi.org/10.1080/07294360701658765.

Humburg, M., de Grip, A., & van der Velden, R. (2017). Which skills protect graduates against a slack labour market? *International Labour Review, 156*(1), 25–43. https://doi.org/10.1111/j.1564-913x.2015.00046.x.

Ibrahim, W., Ibrahim, W., Zoubeidi, T., Marzouk, S., Sweedan, A., & Amer, H. (2022). An online management system for streamlining and enhancing the quality of learning outcomes assessment. *Education and Information Technologies, 27*, 11325–11353.

Jaasma, M.A., & Koper, R.J. (1999). The relationship of student-faculty out-of-class communication to instructor immediacy and trust and to student motivation. *Communication Education, 48*(1), 41–47. https://doi.org/10.1080/03634529909379151.

Jaber, R. & Kennedy, E., (2017). Not the same person anymore: Groupwork, identity and social learning online. *Distance Education, 38*(2), 216–229. https://doi.org/10.1080/01587919.2017.1324732.

Jackson, D. (2014). Testing a model of undergraduate competence in employability skills and its implications for stakeholders. *Journal of Education and Work, 27*(2), 220–242. https://doi.org/10.1080/13639080.2012.718750.

Jackson, D. (2015). Employability skill development in work-integrated learning: Barriers and best practice. *Studies in Higher Education, 40*(2), 350–367. https://doi.org/10.1080/03075079.2013.842221.

Jæger, M.M. (2011). Does cultural capital really affect academic achievement? New evidence from combined sibling and panel data. *Sociology of Education, 84*(4), 281–298. https://doi.org/10.1177/0038040711417010.

Kaur, J., & Sandhu, K.K. (2016). Psychological capital in relation to stress among university students. *Indian Journal of Health and Wellbeing, 7*(3), 323–326. http://www.i-scholar.in/index.php/ijhw/article/view/122134.

Kolb, D.A. (2014). *Experiential Learning: Experience as the Source of Learning and Development.* 2nd Edition. Upper Saddle River, NJ: Pearson Education.

Koppi, T., Sheard, J., Naghdy, F., Chicharo, J., Edwards, S.L., Brookes, W., & Wilson, D.W. (2009). What our ICT graduates really need from us: A perspective from the workplace. In T. Clear & M. Hamilton (eds), *Conferences in Research and Practice in Information Technology Volume 95: Computing Education 2009.* Australia: Australian Computer Society, pp. 101–110.

Lardy, L., Bressoux, P.P., & De Clercq, M. (2022). Achievement of first-year students at the university: A multilevel analysis of the role of background diversity and student engagement. *European Journal of Psychology of Education, 37*(3), 949–969. https://doi.org/10.1007/s10212-021-00570-0.

Larkin, H., & Richardson, B. (2013). Creating high challenge/high support academic environments through constructive alignment: Student outcomes. *Teaching in Higher Education*, *18*(2), 192–204. https://doi.org/10.1080/13562517.2012.696541.

Lewin, K. (1943). Defining the 'field at a given time.' *Psychological Review*, *50*(3), 292–310. https://doi.org/10.1037/h0062738.

Liu, N., & Carless, D. (2006). Peer feedback: The learning element of peer assessment. *Teaching in Higher Education*, *11*(3), 279–290. https:// doi .org/ 10 .1080/ 13562510600680582.

Lueg, R., Lueg, K., & Lauridsen, O. (2016). Aligning seminars with Bologna requirements: Reciprocal peer tutoring, the solo taxonomy and deep learning. *Studies in Higher Education*, *41*(9), 1674–1691. https:// doi .org/ 10 .1080/ 03075079 .2014 .1002832.

Luthans, F., Luthans, K.W., & Luthans, B.C. (2004). Positive psychological capital: Beyond human and social capital. *Business Horizons*, *47*(1), 45–50. https://doi.org/ 10.1016/j.bushor.2003.11.007.

Luthans, F., Youssef, C.M., & Avolio, B.J. (2015). *Psychological Capital and Beyond*. New York: Oxford University Press.

Marton, F., & Säljö, R. (1976). On qualitative differences in learning: Outcome and process. *British Journal of Educational Psychology*, *46*(1), 4–11. https://doi.org/10 .1111/j.2044-8279.1976.tb02980.x.

McGregor, H.A., & Elliot, A.J. (2005). The shame of failure: Examining the link between fear of failure and shame. *Personality and Social Psychology Bulletin*, *31*(2), 218–231. https://doi.org/10.1177/0146167204271420.

Moy, J.W. (2006). Are employers assessing the right traits in hiring? Evidence from Hong Kong companies. *The International Journal of Human Resource Management*, *17*(4), 734–754. https://doi.org/10.1080/09585190600581717.

Murtaugh, P.A., Burns, L.D., & Schuster, J. (1999). Predicting the retention of university students. *Research in Higher Education*, *40*(3), 355–371. https://doi.org/10 .1023/A:1018755201899.

Muuro, M.E., Wagacha, W.P., Kihoro, J.M., & Oboko, R. (2014). Students' perceived challenges in an online collaborative learning environment: A case of higher learning institutions in Nairobi, Kenya. *The International Review of Research in Open and Distributed Learning*, *15*(6). https://doi.org/10.19173/irrodl.v15i6.1768.

Neer, M.R. (1987). The development of an instrument to measure classroom apprehension. *Communication Education*, *36*(2), 154–166. https:// doi .org/ 10 .1080/ 03634528709378656.

Nicholson, L., Putwain, D.W., Connors, L., & Hornby-Atkinson, P. (2013). The key to successful achievement as an undergraduate student: Confidence and realistic expectations? *Studies in Higher Education*, *38*(2), 285–298. https://doi.org/10.1080/ 03075079.2011.585710.

Nicol, D., Thomson, A., & Breslin, C. (2014). Rethinking feedback practices in higher education: A peer review perspective. *Assessment and Evaluation in Higher Education*, *39*(1), 102–122. https://doi.org/10.1080/02602938.2013.795518.

Nicolescu, L., & Paun, C.P. (2009). Relating higher education with the labour market: Graduates' expectations and employers' requirements. *Tertiary Education and Management*, *15*(1), 17–33. https://doi.org/10.1080/13583880802700024.

Norton, L. (2004). Using assessment criteria as learning criteria: A case study in psychology. *Assessment and Evaluation in Higher Education*, *29*(6), 687–702.

Opie, T.R., Livingston, B., Greenberg, D.N., & Murphy, W.M. (2019). Building gender inclusivity: Disentangling the influence of classroom demography on classroom participation. *Higher Education, 77*(1), 37–58. https://doi.org/10.1007/s10734-018 -0245-2.

Osmani, M., Weerakkody, V., Hindi, N., & Eldabi, T. (2019). Graduates employability skills: A review of literature against market demand. *Journal of Education for Business, 94*(7), 423–432. https://doi.org/10.1080/08832323.2018.1545629.

Pande, M., & Bharathi, S.V. (2020). Theoretical foundations of design thinking: A constructivism learning approach to design thinking. *Thinking Skills and Creativity, 36*, 100637. https://doi.org/10.1016/j.tsc.2020.100637.

Parker, A., Halgin, D.S., & Borgatti, S.P. (2016). Dynamics of social capital: Effects of performance feedback on network change. *Organization Studies, 37*(3), 375–397. https://doi.org/10.1177/0170840615613371.

Pather, S., & Dorasamy, N. (2018). The mismatch between first-year students' expectations and experience alongside university access and success: A South African university case study. *Journal of Student Affairs in Africa, 6*(1). https://doi.org/10 .24085/jsaa.v6i1.3065.

Paura, L., & Arhipova, I. (2014). Cause analysis of students' dropout rate in higher education study program. *Procedia – Social and Behavioral Sciences, 109*, 1282–1286. https://doi.org/10.1016/j.sbspro.2013.12.625.

Phillips, D.C. (1995). The good, the bad, and the ugly: The many faces of constructivism. *Educational Researcher, 24*(7), 5–12. https://doi.org/10.3102/0013189x024007005.

Prilleltensky, I. (1997). Values, assumptions, and practices: Assessing the moral implications of psychological discourse and action. *American Psychologist, 52*(5), 517–535. https://doi.org/10.1037/0003-066x.52.5.517.

Reinholz, D. (2016). The assessment cycle: A model for learning through peer assessment. *Assessment and Evaluation in Higher Education, 41*(2), 301–315.

Ren, S., Zhu, Y., & Warner, M. (2011). Human resources, higher education reform and employment opportunities for university graduates in the People's Republic of China. *The International Journal of Human Resource Management, 22*(16), 3429–3446. https://doi.org/10.1080/09585192.2011.586871.

Richardson, J.C., Maeda, Y., Lv, J., & Caskurlu, S. (2017). Social presence in relation to students' satisfaction and learning in the online environment: A meta-analysis. *Computers in Human Behavior, 71*, 402–417. https://doi.org/10.1016/j.chb.2017.02 .001.

Rico-Juan, J.R., Cachero, C., & Macià, H. (2022). Influence of individual versus collaborative peer assessment on score accuracy and learning outcomes in higher education: An empirical study. *Assessment and Evaluation in Higher Education, 47*(4), 570–587. https://doi.org/10.1080/02602938.2021.1955090.

Rissanen, I., Kuusisto, E., Hanhimäki, E., & Tirri, K. (2016). Teachers' implicit meaning systems and their implications for pedagogical thinking and practice: A case study from Finland. *Scandinavian Journal of Educational Research, 62*(4), 487–500. https://doi.org/10.1080/00313831.2016.1258667.

Sakiz, G., Pape, S.J., & Hoy, A.W. (2012). Does perceived teacher affective support matter for middle school students in mathematics classrooms? *Journal of School Psychology, 50*(2), 235–255. https://doi.org/10.1016/j.jsp.2011.10.005.

Scholarios, D., Van der Heijden, B.I.J.M., Van der Schoot, E., Bozionelos, N., Epitropaki, O., Jedrzejowicz, P., Knauth, P., Marzec, I., Mikkelsen, A., & Van der Heijde, C.M. (2008). Employability and the psychological contract in European ICT sector SMEs. *The International Journal of Human Resource Management, 19*(6), 1035–1055. https://doi.org/10.1080/09585190802051337.

Schultz, T.W. (1961). Investment in human capital. *The American Economic Review*, *51*(1), 1–17.

Schweitzer, L., & Stephenson, M. (2008). Charting the challenges and paradoxes of constructivism: A view from professional education. *Teaching in Higher Education*, *13*(5), 583–593. https://doi.org/10.1080/13562510802334947.

Schwinger, M., Wirthwein, L., Lemmer, G., & Steinmayr, R. (2014). Academic self-handicapping and achievement: A meta-analysis. *Journal of Educational Psychology*, *106*(3), 744–761. https://doi.org/10.1037/a0035832.

Shcheglova, I., Gorbunova, E., & Chirikov, I. (2020). The role of the first-year experience in student attrition. *Quality in Higher Education*, *26*(3), 307–322. https://doi .org/10.1080/13538322.2020.1815285.

Skinner, K. (2014). Bridging gaps and jumping through hoops: First-year History students' expectations and perceptions of assessment and feedback in a research-intensive UK university. *Arts and Humanities in Higher Education*, *13*(4), 359–376. https:// doi.org/10.1177/1474022214531502.

Sumsion, J., & Goodfellow, J. (2004). Identifying generic skills through curriculum mapping: A critical evaluation. *Higher Education Research and Development*, *23*(3), 329–346. https://doi.org/10.1080/0729436042000235436.

Sun, H., & Richardson, J.T.E. (2012). Perceptions of quality and approaches to studying in higher education: A comparative study of Chinese and British postgraduate students at six British business schools. *Higher Education*, *63*(3), 299–316. https:// doi.org/10.1007/s10734-011-9442-y.

Tholen, G. (2014). *The Changing Nature of the Graduate Labour Market: Media, Policy and Political Discourses in the UK*. Basingstoke: Palgrave Macmillan. https://doi.org/10.1057/9781137479075.

Thomas, K., Ochrach, C., Phillips, B., & Tansey, T. (2021). Social justice as an organizational identity: An inductive case study examining the role of diversity and inclusivity initiatives in corporate climate and productivity. *Journal of Business Diversity*, *21*(4), 31–43. https://go.openathens.net/redirector/leeds.ac.uk?url=https:// www .proquest .com/ scholarly -journals/ social -justice -as -organizational -identity/ docview/2608160365/se-2.

Thurner, V., & Böttcher, A. (2022). An architectural concept for didactics that integrates technology into teaching, learning and assessment. In M.E. Auer, A. Pester, & D. May (eds), *Learning with Technologies and Technologies in Learning*. Lecture Notes in Networks and Systems, vol. 456. Cham: Springer, pp. 391–418. https://doi .org/10.1007/978-3-031-04286-7_19.

Treleaven, L., & Voola, R. (2008). Integrating the development of graduate attributes through constructive alignment. *Journal of Marketing Education*, *30*(2), 160–173. https://doi.org/10.1177/0273475308319352.

Van Bergen, P., & Parsell, M. (2019). Comparing radical, social and psychological constructivism in Australian higher education: A psycho-philosophical perspective. *Australian Educational Researcher*, *46*(1), 41–58. https://doi.org/10.1007/s13384 -018-0285-8.

Vryonides, M., & Gouvias, D. (2012). Parents' aspirations for their children's educational and occupational prospects in Greece: The role of social class. *International Journal of Educational Research*, *53*, 319–329. https://doi.org/10.1016/j.ijer.2012 .04.005.

Wang, X., Su, Y., Cheung, S., Wong, E., & Kwong, T. (2013). An exploration of Biggs' constructive alignment in course design and its impact on students' learning approaches. *Assessment and Evaluation in Higher Education*, *38*(4), 477–491. https://doi.org/10.1080/02602938.2012.658018.

Webster, D.M. (2016). Listening to the voice of dyslexic students at a small, vocational higher education institution to promote successful inclusive practice in the 21st century. *International Journal of Learning and Teaching*, *2*, 78–86. https://doi.org/10.18178/ijlt.2.1.

Wells, G. (1999). Using L1 to master L2: A response to Antón and DiCamilla's 'Socio-Cognitive Functions of L1 Collaborative Interaction in the L2 Classroom.' *The Modern Language Journal*, *83*(2), 248–254. https://doi.org/10.1111/0026-7902.00019.

Wenger, E., McDermott, R.A., & Snyder, W.M. (2002). *Cultivating Communities of Practice: A Guide to Managing Knowledge*. Boston, MA: Harvard Business Press.

White, J.W. (2011). Resistance to classroom participation: Minority students, academic discourse, cultural conflicts, and issues of representation in whole class discussions. *Journal of Language Identity and Education*, *10*(4), 250–265. https://doi.org/10.1080/15348458.2011.598128.

Wilson Review. (2012). *A Review of Business–University Collaboration*. [Online] Accessed 6 August 2023. Available from: https://assets.publishing.service.gov.uk/government/uploads/system/uploads/attachment_data/file/32383/12-610-wilson-review-business-university-collaboration.pdf.

Woodward, K. (2003). *Understanding Identity*. London: Bloomsbury Academic.

Yazici, H. (2004). Student perceptions of collaborative learning in operations management classes. *Journal of Education for Business*, *80*(2), 110–118. https://doi.org/10.3200/joeb.80.2.110-118.

Zander, L., Brouwer, J., Jansen, E., Crayen, C., & Hannover, B. (2018). Academic self-efficacy, growth mindsets, and university students' integration in academic and social support networks. *Learning and Individual Differences*, *62*, 98–107. https://doi.org/10.1016/j.lindif.2018.01.012.

Zimmermann, P.A., Stallings, L., Pierce, R.L., & Largent, D.L. (2018). Classroom interaction redefined: Multidisciplinary perspectives on moving beyond traditional classroom spaces to promote student engagement. *Journal of Learning Spaces*, *7*(1), 45–61. http://files.eric.ed.gov/fulltext/EJ1195242.pdf.

Index